PLANTS of Waterton- Glacier National Parks
and The Northern Rockies

Richard J. Shaw
Professor of Botany
Utah State University
Logan, Utah

and

Danny On
Silviculturist
Flathead National Forest
Montana

MOUNTAIN PRESS PUBLISHING COMPANY
MISSOULA, 1979

© Copyright 1979

Mountain Press Publishing Company

2nd Printing, 1981

3rd Printing, June 1983

4th Printing , July 1987

5th Printing, May 1989

Library of Congress Cataloging in Publication Data

On, Danny
   Plants of Waterton-Glacier National Parks
   Bibliography: p.
   Includes index.
   1. Botany—Montana—Glacier National Park.
   2. Botany—Alberta—Waterton Lakes National Park.
   3. Glacier National Park.   4. Waterton Lakes National
Park, Alta.   I. Shaw, Richard J., joint author.
II. Title.
QK171.05   581.9'786'52   79-9912
ISBN 0-87842-114-9

Picking wildflowers or collecting specimens of animals, trees or minerals in all National Parks and Monuments is prohibited without special permission from the park superintendent. Study the plants where they grow, take home photographs of them, but leave them for the enjoyment of those who will follow.

Cover—Lewis Monkeyflower
Photo by Danny On

Mountain Press Publishing Company
2016 Strand Avenue • P.O. Box 2399
Missoula, Montana 59806
Phone (406) 728-1900

$8.95

Photo by Mel Ruder

Dedication

It has been a great honor to have worked with Danny On and I wish to dedicate this book to him. Danny was a respected silviculturist with the U.S. Forest Service and was well known as a photographer who immortalized the outdoors. He had a keen interest in the preservation of our National Parks and participated as a member of the board of directors of Glacier Natural History Association. His many accomplishments as a professional forester, conservationist and photographer won him the respect of many friends.

R.J.S.

Acknowledgments

We offer our sincere thanks to Edwin L. Rothfuss, Chief Naturalist of Glacier National Park and to the Glacier Natural History Association. Without their encouragement and support, this book could not have been completed.

Betsy Graff gave considerable assistance in supplying information concerning the history of plants in the two parks. Dr. Phyllis Marsh, Geologist for Flathead National Forest, and Dr. Robert Hall, Plant Ecologist at Glacier National Park, made helpful suggestions with the manuscript.

Jerry DeSanto, the Sub-district Ranger of the North Fork, made a major contribution in the final phases of writing by supplying information about species distribution.

Margaret Mortensen, Robert Kretzer and Glacier National Park kindly loaned photographs, and credits for these are given in the text. The remaining photographs were taken by the authors.

Special appreciation goes to Marion Shaw who spent many hours waiting for photographs to be taken and for typing the manuscript.

Contents

METRIC SYSTEM TABLE

 1 mm. = approx. 1/25 of an inch
10 mm. = 1 cm. (approx. 2/5 of an inch)
10 cm. = 1 dm. (approx. 4 inches)
10 dm. = 1 m. (approx. 40 inches)

Introduction

The purpose of this plant book is to provide park visitors who lack botanical training a source of information about the fascinating vegetation that blankets the surface of two of North America's most beautiful National Parks. It is the result of many years of study of the plants of the region and consideration of what the visitor wants to know about "that plant." It is hoped that the photographs in color, non-technical descriptions, and convenient size will make the book useful to the backpacker, mountain climber and highway traveler.

A 1974 checklist of Glacier National Park includes over 1,000 species of vascular plants that inhabit an incredible number of diverse habitats. Of these plants 220 species have been chosen for illustration and description. It will be apparent that many admirable species have been neglected, but an attempt has been made to include wildflowers, several of the tree species, and the majority of shrubs (except for numerous willow species) which represent a view of 88 families within the boundaries of the two parks. The combined size of Waterton-Glacier International Peace Park exceeds 2,000 square miles (5202 sq. km.) and includes an awe-inspiring landscape of glacier carved mountains, ranging from 3,110 to 10,466 feet (948 to 3190 m.), about 50 small glaciers, mountain lakes of many sizes, and river drainages flowing to the Pacific Ocean, the Gulf of Mexico, and the Hudson Bay. This area, slightly smaller than the state of Delaware, has a cold, Alaska-type climate with deep, drifting snow and a growing season of approximately 60 frost-free days.

Arrangement of the Plants

The book begins with three species of ferns and fern allies, and the trees follow with emphasis on conifers. Shrubs and herbaceous plants are in separate sections. Herbaceous plants are in an artificial arrangement according to flower color. While this is a practical system, it is advisable to check more than one section if color deviation is suspected. Five color groups have been selected as follows: (1) green to white, including cream, (2) yellow to orange, (3) pink to red, (4) blue to purple, including lavender, and (5) brown, including reddish-brown. Arbitrary decisions had to be made between groups (3) and (4) because some flower colors are intermediate between pink and purple and show a range of variation at different stages of maturation or even on the same inflorescence.

Common Names

Long ago, botanists reached international agreement that there should be only one valid scientific name for each plant species, but no such action has been taken concerning common names. Indeed, it is unlikely that such action will be taken. Consequently, a multiplicity of common names may occur for many species, often varying from state to state and country to country. For example, *Erythronium grandiflorum* in Utah is most often called dogtooth violet, yet in Colorado and Montana it is called glacier lily. To solve the problem in this volume, the authors have often included several names and tried to follow the names applied by recent identification manuals (see selected references).

Brief History of Plants of Waterton-Glacier National Parks

Field and laboratory studies conducted in both parks in the last three decades tell a story of vegetation spanning millions of years. This vegetational history will never be completely understood, but because of thousands of feet of ancient mudstones, limestones and sandstones, there is evidence of sedimentary environments that were alternately wet and dry. Plant fossils, including remains of blue-green algae which represents the most primitive of all living organisms, are abundant in some layers.

Monkeyflowers   DO

The ancient sedimentary layers of the parks remained essentially undisturbed for the better part of a billion years. Then, about 70 million years ago, the recurring seas retreated for the last time as crustal upheavals raised the Rocky Mountain region several thousand feet and the accumulated sediments in the region of Waterton-Glacier Parks began to slide off the uplift. The present mountains of the parks were carved by erosion from a single great slab of this ancient sedimentary rock that slid in an easterly direction and rode over relatively soft deposits of mud and sand.

For many millions of years after the main uplift of the Rocky Mountains, the region had a dry climate. Approximately three million years ago, the climate changed and the first of at least four major ice ages began. Glaciers shaped the mountain valleys and sculptured the peaks. Even the continental ice cap, which was spreading over much of Canada, extended into the north eastern portion of Waterton Lakes National Park. Now the glaciers have almost melted and other processes are reshaping the landscape.

With its highest peaks outlining the Continental Divide, the Rocky Mountain Range forms a formidable weather barrier in this region. Thus Waterton-Glacier, being part of this barrier, is split into quite different environments. Glacier's western half experiences moderate temperatures and is generally moist, characterized by heavy snows during winter, and rain and snow during spring and fall. Continental air masses influence the climate on the eastern portion of the parks with colder temperatures and less precipitation.

Waterton-Glacier's present vegetation mosaic has developed since the last ice retreat about 10,000 years ago. At the high elevations extreme climate and soil development have limited the plant communities. At low elevations, however, a more moderate climate has allowed a succession of plant communities leading to a forest cover that

Wildflowers near St. Mary   DO

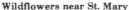

has been present for thousands of years. As the ice receded from these low slopes, lodgepole pine invaded, accompanied by lesser quantities of other pine species, spruce, fir, and Douglas-fir. Forest fires have probably always had some role in patterning these forests. Early descriptions of Glacier's landscape emphasize the many stages of forest growth after fire.

Forests on the east side alternate with prairies, moist meadows, shrub communities, aspen groves, scattered limber pine, and rock outcrops. The subalpine forest is composed of whitebark pine and subalpine fir. At low elevations Douglas-fir, spruce and subalpine fir are characteristic of mature forests, but much of the area is covered by successional lodgepole pine. A number of descriptions of the east side reveal that man-caused and natural fire played an important role in the landscape that now prevails.

The low areas of Glacier's west side appear at first to be homogeneous forests broken by occasional grasslands. This forest actually changes with variations in a number of factors such as precipitation, temperature, soil, topography and the disturbances of fire and flood. Cottonwood and spruce dominate wet valley bottom sites while ponderosa pine, lodgepole pine and Douglas-fir characterize the warmest and driest forest sites. Western red cedar, western hemlock, grand fir, spruce, subalpine fir, and Pacific yew inhabit moist sites.

Most forest stands have varying numbers of western larch, western white pine, and lodgepole pine, all of which are known as fire dependent species. Almost pure stands of lodgepole pine are located on moderately dry sites that have been burned by wildfires within the past 100 years. The stands are being attacked by a major epidemic of the mountain pine beetle.

Although about two-thirds of Glacier's land area is forested, it is the spectacular alpine tundra, high peaks, bare rock, and snowfields which catch the eye. The alpine landscape supports a variety of vegetation including lichens, sparse perennial herbs, lush meadows, prostrate shrubs, and "krumholz" forests. The latter forest has isolated patches of alpine larch and subalpine fir. The incessant winds and driving ice crystals give the trees a distorted form, hence the name "krumholz" meaning crooked wood.

Additional studies of the biotic elements encompassed within the park's boundaries will surely expand our fascinating view of plant migration, extinction and evolution.

Hints on Photographing Wildflowers

The majority of wildflowers can be photographed in lively color with today's moderately priced automatic cameras equipped with attachable close-up lenses. Such a lens or series of lenses (which usually retail between $15.00 to $40.00) will allow you to shoot as close as six inches from the blossoms. If you are quite serious about flower photography, consider the purchase of a 35 mm, single lens reflex camera with a 50 mm macro lens. When the f stop is closed down to f 22, the greatest depth of field will be achieved, and this is very important in a situation where the flowers are in a cluster or you wish to show detail deep within a tubular corolla. A small, portable tripod will provide the support necessary for speeds as slow as ⅛ or ¼ second. If working from a car, a larger format camera is desirable, such as a 2¼-inch Mamiya or Hasselblad or even a 4x5-inch view camera.

A variety of color film is available from the Kodachrome 25 and 64 to High Speed Ectachrome. Perhaps Kodachrome 64 combines the best advantages of superb color, sharpness and reasonable film speed.

You will have better results when you project your slides if you have taken time to compose each shot for maximum detail and appropriate background. Backgrounds may be provided by natural shadows or even blue sky if a low shooting angle is possible. Natural objects in the plant's environment, such as a downed log, may be helpful and often give a feeling of naturalness. However, there may be times when you want to show accurate flower structure with maximum contrast, and this is the time to utilize an artificial background. A piece of black velvet or paper held behind the flower may be all that is needed.

A good approach to the art includes the concept that you are going to create a portfolio of shots for each species. This means patience to wait until the breeze dies down, patience to outlast the insects, hot sun and those curious strangers that want to know what you are doing. Finally, take several pictures of the choice subjects using different angles, exposure times and vertical and horizontal views. Remember, a photographic effort on plants will be rewarding for years to come.

Size of Plants

Scale of each illustration is indicated to the right of the name, thus:

Woodland Pine Drops ⅞X

means that the illustration is seven-eights as large as the original plant. The actual size of the average plant will then be a little larger than the illustration. (Similarly, the picture of **Woodnymph 1X** is actual life-size.)

Common Horsetail

Equisetum arvense

Horsetails are among the oldest vascular plants with a history going back millions of years. This species is widely distributed in North America and tends to inhabit wet soils. An underground stem gives rise to two kinds of aerial stems. One appears in the spring and is usually pale brown with a terminal, spore-bearing strobilus. The other aerial branch is sterile, green and has whorls of small branches at the nodes. The stems contain silica particles which give them an abrasive quality, and many pioneers used them to scour pans. This is a favorite bear food, especially in the spring in the North Fork Valley.

Rockbrake; Parsley Fern

Cryptogramma crispa

The leaves are densely tufted on a short rhizome, and this delicate fern can be readily recognized by the short, sterile fronds mixed with the taller fertile fronds. It also helps to look at the small leaflets of the fertile fronds with a hand lens and note the clusters of sporangia protected by the recurved leaf margins. Fern species inhabit a variety of habitats from very wet to very dry situations and rockbrake is one which is adapted to calcareous cliff crevices and talus of the mountains. A second species, *C. stelleri*, is often found by waterfalls or in moist crevices in shaded canyons.

Bracken Fern

Pteridium aquilinum

The largest fern species of the parks is widely distributed in North America, Europe, Asia and the Southern Hemisphere. The plant begins the growth of fronds in June and they remain green until late September. All portions of the fronds are poisonous to livestock, especially cattle and horses. However, several edible plant books recommend the eating of young fronds when they are still shaped like fiddlenecks. Some authors of plant toxicology warn that this fern contains a carcinogen and should never be eaten. The plant inhabits burned-over sites in forests which provide shade and adequate moisture. Certainly the lush beauty of the fronds adds much to the wilderness scene.

Common Horsetail ¾x

Rockbrake ¾x

Bracken Fern 1x

Subalpine Fir

Abies lasiocarpa

Perhaps the best way to identify this conifer from a distance is to watch for its long, slender, narrowly conical crown. When close to this species, one can see that its flat, flexible needles and erect cones distinguish it from all other evergreens except grand fir. Although subalpine fir is a relatively small tree and of little commercial importance, it is the most widely distributed fir in western North America. As the name implies, this species grows up to timberline at 7,000 feet where it may grow very shrublike. Within the parks, it is associated with Englemann spruce and lodgepole pine, especially tolerating the shade of the latter species. At lower elevations subalpine fir indicates frost pockets. The smooth, gray bark of young trees is unique because of the many lens-shaped blisters, often up to 1 inch or more in length, which are filled with a sticky resin. On older trees the bark is little broken except for shallow cracks near the base of the trunk. As a result of heavy snows, the lower branches often become rooted, thus forming a circle of smaller trees. Such a colony is called a snowmat of subalpine fir. The squirrels tear open the large cones when the seeds ripen in September.

Grand Fir

Abies grandis

The reproductive organs of firs are similar to those of pines with separate male and female cones on the same tree. The female cones, however, stand erect on the upper branches, and at maturity, the ovuliferous scales and seeds are shed from the central cone axis which remains upright on the tree for months afterwards. Grand fir is usually found at relatively low elevations in well-drained alluvial soils and is mixed with Douglas-fir, western red cedar and western hemlock. The grayish-brown bark on young trees is blotched with resin blisters and with age, becomes scaly and broken into dark gray, flat ridges. The wood is light and relatively low in strength. The crown of mature trees is rounded and dome-like.

Engelmann Spruce

Picea engelmannii

The spruces have narrow crowns of many pliable branches and long, straight trunks with scaly bark. The needles and cones are its distinguishing features. Remember that the word spruce begins with "s" and the single needles are square in cross-section and sharp to the touch. Check the square in cross-section characteristic by rolling a needle between thumb and forefinger. The reproductive organs are similar to those of pines with the pollen and seed cones on the same tree. The seed cones are narrowly oval and have finely toothed, papery scales. Length of these cones varies from 1 to 3 inches. The wood of these trees is moderately strong and has little contrast between heartwood and sapwood. The white spruce (*Picea glauca*) also occurs in the parks and hybrids between the two species are widespread. White spruce characteristics are not very evident at higher elevations. The cone scales of white spruce have smooth margins and its twigs are normally without the fine, short hairs (pubescence) characteristic of Engelmann spruce.

Subalpine Fir ½x RJS

Grand Fir DO

Englemann Spruce RJS

Englemann Spruce ½x RJS

Douglas-fir

Pine Family

Pseudotsuga menziesii

Douglas-fir is widely distributed in the Western states, reaching its largest size in the coastal region of Washington and Oregon. In the parks of the Rocky Mountain Region, we have a smaller, slower growing variety. This species bears strong resemblance to spruce, fir, and hemlock, thus botanists gave it a generic name of *Pseudotsuga* (false hemlock). The flat, flexible needles are borne singly and grow around the branch giving it a full appearance. The seed cones set the tree apart from the true firs because they hang down and do not disintegrate on the tree as they do in the case of the firs. The best distinguishing feature of this species is found in the female cone. Between the cone scales are prominent three-pronged bracts. As the color plate indicates, these "Neptune's tridents" appear in both early and mature stages of cone development. On the same tree, bright red male cones appear in the early spring, but fall off as soon as the pollen is shed. The bark on older individuals is reddish-brown and deeply fissured, often up to 5 inches or more in thickness. Because of the thick bark, some individuals may survive hot forest fires.

Western Larch

Pine Family

Larix occidentalis

The members of this genus differ from all other native conifers in not retaining their foliage over the winter. Each year their leaves turn yellow late in the fall and are shed before winter sets in. The slender, flexible leaves, borne in tuft-like clusters of 10-30, are located on short, spur-like branches. The western larch is the largest of the larches — up to 38 inches in diameter at breast height and heights of 100 to 180 feet are common. Some individuals are possibly 700 years old. This species is very intolerant of shade and requires a well-lighted habitat for its full development. A much smaller species, the alpine larch (*L. lyallii*) is found at altitudes of 6000 to 7000 feet on rocky and gravelly soils. Both species have male and female cones on the same tree. A small area of alpine larch is located in Preston Park, along the trail to Siyeh Pass.

Douglas-fir RJS

Douglas-fir ¾x DO

Western Larch DO

Western Larch 1x DO

Western Yew
Taxus brevifolia
In northern Idaho and the West Coast states, western yew is usually a small tree 15 to 25 feet high. It grows best on moist slopes and flats along streams. In G.N.P. it is reduced to a low-spreading shrub. Species of this genus differ from other gymnosperms in having a single dark-bluish seed, ⅓-inch long, surrounded by a red, fleshy, cup-shaped covering. The seed with the covering is about the size of a pea. The plants have sharp-pointed, needle-like leaves that have a distinct, short petiole at the base and tend to spread in two ranks. The wood has been prized for bows used in archery. The leaves and seeds are highly poisonous to livestock and man.

Western Hemlock
Tsuga heterophylla
Hemlocks are handsome trees with soft, delicate foliage and a drooping leader (stem tip). The linear needles are flat and have a blunt tip. They grow from small, persistent woody swellings similar to the more prominent woody pegs of spruces. Leaves and branches suggest the Douglas-fir, but *Tsuga* differs from *Pseudotsuga* in having cones with concealed bracts. In western hemlock the cones are about ¾-inch long and spread widely on opening to release seed in autumn. This species seldom grows in pure stands and is often mixed with western larch, western white pine, Douglas-fir, and western red cedar. The seedlings can tolerate shading and are commonly found on decaying logs. Not being able to develop in the shade, most of its associated tree species depend on wildfires to create favorable conditions for reproduction. Without wildfires western hemlock continues to reproduce in the shade and dominate moist forest sites. This process can be observed along the north end of Lake McDonald.

Western Red Cedar
Thuja plicata
The name "cedar" is applied to several genera of gymnosperms which have scale-like foliage and aromatic wood. This particular cedar is common in the McDonald Valley and a small stand occurs in the Quartz drainage on the Quartz Creek Trail near the head of Lower Quartz Lake. It is also found at other scattered locations in the North Fork Valley, i.e. Red Meadow Creek. It seldom grows in pure stands but generally mixes with other species. The bark is fibrous, reddish-brown and vertically ridged. The very light wood is straight-grained and resistant to decay. The oval cones are up to ¾-inch in length and have cone-scales with sharp points near the tip. Western red cedar is a long-lived species. One specimen was 800 years old when it was cut. The Indians of the Pacific Northwest utilized these trees for canoes, lodges and totem poles. The largest specimen in G.N.P. is over 4 feet in diameter and 100 feet high.

Western Yew 1½x   DO

Western Hemlock   GNP

Western Red Cedar   DO

Western Red Cedar 1x   GNP

Rocky Mountain Juniper

Cypress Family

Juniperus scopulorum

Rocky Mountain juniper is prevalent in western United States and Canada and does well in dry valleys and hills and along shores of streams and lakes where there is little competition from other trees. It is generally a bushy shrub or small tree, often with several trunks. The leaves are mostly scale-like and opposite; however, some juvenile, needle-like leaves are often persistent until near maturity of the trees. Some individuals produce only pollen cones while others produce only seed cones. The seed cones mature into pea-sized, fleshy, berry-like structures with wingless seeds. The Indians ate the seed cones in late summer or fall. This tree grows along North Fork Valley in dry places. The largest known individual has a 33-inch diameter at breast height and is located 3 miles north of Polebridge.

Western White Pine

Pine Family

Pinus monticola

Western white pine grows on a wide variety of soils, but thrives best on well-drained soils in moist valleys and gentle slopes with northern exposures. It may form pure stands, but is usually mixed with other species. The needles are rough to the touch and are in groups of fives, 2-4 inches long. The bark is relatively thin and grayish when young, becoming darker with age. On older trunks, the bark forms squarish, scaly plates. The pale yellow pollen cones are in clusters and release their pollen in early June. The seed cones are 5-10 inches long, usually slightly curved and covered with resin. Like the lodgepole pine, this tree is known as a fire dependent species. In the McDonald Valley some large specimens of this species reach 170 feet high and have a breast high diameter of 5 feet.

Ponderosa Pine; Yellow Pine

Pine Family

Pinus ponderosa

The ponderosa pine is the most widely distributed species of *Pinus* in North America, extending from Canada south to Mexico. On dry sites it produces forests of openly spaced trees which have long had commercial value. The needles are usually three to a bundle and persist on the tree for about 3 to 5 years. The bark is especially helpful in distinguishing it from other species. It is 2-4 inches thick, cinnamon red and divided by fissures into broad plates. Some have said they can detect the odor of cinnamon in the bark. Indians of Montana, Idaho, and British Columbia ate the seeds of this species by crushing them into a meal which was made into bread. They also ate the inner bark as a survival food. Being very intolerant of shade, ponderosa pine, under natural conditions, requires wildfires to maintain its presence on sites that are suitable for other tree species. In G.N.P. it is located mainly up the North Fork of the Flathead River.

ocky Mountain Juniper   RJS

Western White Pine   DO

onderosa Pine   DO

Ponderosa Pine   ½x   DO

Whitebark Pine

Pine Family

Pinus albicaulis

Since this species is often confused with the limber pine, it would be well to compare the color and length of the seed cones of both species. Whitebark pine seed cones are short (ranging from 2 to 3½ inches long) and remain purple to maturity. In contrast, the limber pine bears seed cones which are longer (ranging from 4 to 8 inches) and remain green until maturity and then turn brown. The bark of whitebark seedlings is covered with a fine white coating, and the larger trunks sometimes have a whitish cast. Because of this, the scientific name *Pinus albicaulis* has been applied and means literally "the pine with the white stem." This species is important in subalpine zones from 6,000 to 7,000 feet, especially where mountain soils are shallow. When exposed to strong winds, it often assumes the habit of a shrub with wide-spreading, twisted branches. The seed cones fall at maturity but are seldom seen on the ground because birds, rodents and grizzly bears feed upon the seeds. There is a dense stand of these trees near Old Man Lake. Some huge trees (one 54 inches at breast height) occur on benches west of Boulder Pass.

Limber Pine

Pine Family

Pinus flexilis

This five-needled pine is seldom found in pure stands, but is more often found as a lone individual on the dry, rocky moraines. The young branches of this tree are very flexible and can be tied in knots without breaking. This peculiar characteristic is of advantage in withstanding the severe winds and is also responsible for both the common and scientific names. In June this species is conspicuous because of its numerous reddish clusters of pollen-bearing cones. The seed-bearing cones (up to six inches long) produce large seed crops at irregular intervals and these are sought by the Clark's Nutcracker which serves as an important agent of dispersal. Each needle is 1½ to 3 inches long, and closely pressed into clusters of five. Such needle clusters often remain on the branches for five to six years. This is a small tree, 30 to 45 feet in height, and 1 to 3 feet in diameter. On old trees, some of the branches become very long, sometimes longer than the height of the tree. This species can be found near Many Glacier and St. Mary. Many picturesque examples grow above Two Medicine on the Mt. Henry Trail.

Whitebark Pine   RJS

Whitebark Pine   ½x   RJS

Limber Pine   ¼x   RJS

Limber Pine   RJS

Lodgepole Pine

Pinus contorta

Of the five species of pines found in the two parks, this is the most common, and the only one with two needles in a cluster. It is a small tree which seldom gets over 75 feet high. When it grows in dense stands, it is characteristically tall and slender, losing the lower branches as they become shaded. If the individual trees are widely spaced, they become quite bushy and densely branched. The lodgepole pine seedlings grow quickly in mineral soil of a fire-cleaned area or in any kind of a disturbed site, particularly road side cuts. The mountain pine bark beetle is the most serious threat to this species since the larvae of the beetle bore under the bark and eventually girdle the tree. Up to 40 to 50 percent of the trees over six inches in diameter have succumbed to the beetle in some areas and nearly 200,000 acres in North Fork area have been affected. Other threats to its existence include the dwarf mistletoe and the comandra rust. The western Indians used the slender trunks of the small trees as a framework for their teepees or lodges, hence the common name, lodgepole pine. From the color plate it is possible to recognize the mature male cones which produce great quantities of pollen in June, the young, green female cone, and the brown, fully-matured female cone containing seeds.

Common Juniper

Juniperus communis

This widely distributed species is to be found across North America, Europe and Asia. Like other junipers, it is easily distinguished by the soft, blue, berry-like fruit. These are not true berries but modified cones whose scales are relished by birds, but the seeds inside are not digested and pass through the digestive tract. For this reason, junipers have a wide distribution. Common juniper is a spreading, creeping shrub, seldom over three feet in height. The sharp-pointed, awl-like needles are in groups of three, ⅜ to ½ inch long. Where the leaf joins the branch, there is a definite constriction. Rocky Mountain juniper (*J. scopulorum*) differs from the common juniper in being a small tree and having scale-like leaves appressed to the twigs. Creeping juniper (*J. horizontalis*) has very long, wide-spreading branches that trail over the ground, plus leaves which are scale-like. The common juniper can be seen along Sun Point self-guiding trail.

Lodgepole Pine RJS

Lodgepole Pine ¾x RJS

Common Juniper 1x RJS

Black Cottonwood

Willow Family

Populus trichocarpa

The black cottonwood is the largest broadleaved tree in the two parks; in fact, along lakes and drainage bottoms, some specimens attain heights of 90 to 120 feet and diameters of 3 to 4 feet. The distinguishing features which set this tree apart are the sticky resin on the buds, the large, broadly ovate leaves which are often up to 5 inches in length, and the deeply furrowed gray bark. The leaves are finely toothed at the margin, dark green on the upper surface and whitish underneath. Flowers of both sexes are borne separately on different trees. By August the more loosely flowered pistillate catkins are 6 to 11 inches long with pointed capsules. The tiny fragile seeds have attached fluffy fibers which carry them long distances. Cottonwoods also reproduce from stumps and root sprouts. The deeply fissured bark of mature trees is 2 to 3 inches thick and provides protection against fire. This species grows mostly on loose, porous, sandy or gravelly soils. The largest known tree of this species in G.N.P. is 68 inches in diameter at breast height and occurs near Quartz Creek Bridge on the North Fork Truck Trail.

Quaking Aspen; Trembling Aspen

Willow Family

Populus tremuloides

The vernacular name, quaking aspen, is traceable to the leaves which move in the slightest breeze. This almost incessant trembling of the leaves is due to the slender, flattened petioles. *Populus tremuloides* is one of the most common broad-leaved trees in the two parks. In fact, it is one of the most widely distributed trees in North America. In most of the Rocky Mountain Region its reproduction is by means of shoots which arise from the shallow root system. As a result of fire or logging, the trembling aspen may produce these shoots or suckers in great abundance. The inconspicuous flowers appear in the spring before the leaves appear. The wind-borne seeds are mature by the time the leaves are fully grown. Horizontal ridges and scars mark the thin, almost white or yellowish-green bark. Bases of old trees are roughened and black. This successful species is found on many soil types, but it makes its best growth on well-drained sandy or gravelly loams. Leaf mining insects are especially common on the leaves of aspen. The larva of the leaf miner lives and feeds between the two epidermal layers of the leaf. After a period of dormancy, a small moth emerges from the pupa. Aspen stands are extensive along roads on the east side of G.N.P. at St. Mary, Two Medicine and Swiftcurrent valleys.

Black Cottonwood RJS

Black Cottonwood ¾x RJS

Quaking Aspen RJS

Quaking Aspen 2x RJS

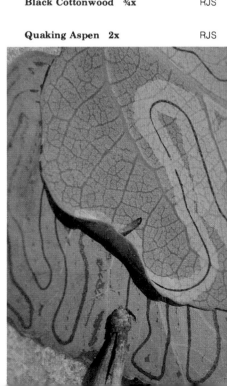

Western Serviceberry; Saskatoon Rose Family
Amelanchier alnifolia

This rosaceous shrub species is often divided into several poorly defined varieties, but the delicate white flowers make it easy to recognize. The apple-like fruits are ⅜ to ½ inch in diameter, becoming dark purple at maturity. The juicy, sweet fruits are sought by many songbirds, but they are more important food to mammals. Squirrels, chipmunks and even bears seem to relish the seedy fruits. Deer, elk and moose are particularly fond of the foliage and twigs. Indians collected, dried and stored the fruits for winter food. They made a type of pemmican of pounded fruits and dried meat to be carried on long trips. These berries are used for jams and jellies, but they are not as popular as the huckleberries. Growing at the edge of grasslands to high mountain forests, this is one of the most widespread shrubs in the northern Rockies. Additional common names for this plant include: Juneberry, sarviceberry and shadbush.

Bearberry; Kinnikinick Heath Family
Arctostaphylos uva-ursi

This trailing, evergreen shrub belongs to the group known as manzanita. It is the only manzanita found outside of western North America. Like other members of this group, bearberry has the characteristic reddish-brown bark and smooth, leathery leaves. The white or pinkish flowers are bell-shaped and form in clusters at the ends of the stems. Later in the season the flowers give place to bright red berries which are a favorite food of bears and grouse. The common name, kinnikinick, comes from an Indian expression referring to the use of the leaves and bark of this species with or in place of tobacco. Look for this shrub on gravel terraces and in open coniferous woods; sometimes growing above timberline. Look for the mats of this shrub on cut slopes along roads near St. Mary Lake. It is abundant on low to mid slopes near Many Glacier.

Western Serviceberry   1x   DO

Western Serviceberry   ¾x   RJS

Bearberry   2x   DO

Bearberry   ¾x   RJS

Orange Honeysuckle
Honeysuckle Family

Lonicera ciliosa

This trailing or climbing woody vine is the showiest of our native honeysuckles. The tubular flowers (over 1¼ inches long) occur in clusters in a terminal cup which is really a pair of fused leaves. Within the tubular corolla there are 5 pubescent stamens. The vivid orange or sometimes yellow blossoms have become adapted for pollination chiefly by hummingbirds. This kind of pollinator, however, means that no scent is present. In the fall the withering flowers give way to bright red berries. Sometimes this climbing shrub may reach 20 feet high on the branches of small conifers. Look for this attractive shrub in moist soil of canyons and hillsides.

Devil's Club
Ginseng Family

Oplopanax horridum

Handsome waxy, red berries and enormous leaves up to 15 inches broad make this shrub quite unmistakable. The stems and leaves are armed with sharp yellow spines and many hikers are aware of the scratches they can inflict. The small greenish-white flowers occur in large clusters in June and later form attractive berries in July and August. This "barbed wire" plant occurs in moist wooded areas especially along small streams. The leaves are deciduous and the stems can reach a height of 10 feet. Some plants are growing along the Trail of the Cedars, near Avalanche Campground. It also occurs in Waterton Valley.

Arctic Willow
Willow Family

Salix arctica

About 75 species of willows grow in North America and at least 20 species survive in the two parks. This circumboreal species occupies a variety of tundra sites from well-drained sandy soils to the shores of alpine lakes. The willows are dioecious, meaning that male and female flowers are on different individuals. The inflorescence pictured is a cluster of male or staminate flowers. The fruits are small pods that split into 2 parts, releasing minute seeds surrounded by tufts of long, white silky hairs. The buds, leaves and twigs of willows are eaten by a variety of wildlife. The tiny buds of arctic willow are eaten by ptarmigans.

Blue Clematis; Virginsbower
Buttercup Family

Clematis columbiana

This woody clematis is one of the few climbing vines of the two parks. The leaf stalks or petioles act like tendrils and attach themselves to large shrubs and small trees. The flowers lack true petals, but are conspicuous because of the blue to lavender petal-like sepals and numerous stamens. The 4 sepals are lanceolate and 1½ to 2 inches long and attractively accented by darker veins. The fruits which develop from numerous pistils have long, fuzzy styles. These feathery styles aid in scattering the 1-seeded achenes. The generic name, *Clematis*, is derived from the Greek *klemma* meaning a vine-branch. This species is common in North Fork and blooms the first week of May.

Orange Honeysuckle ¾x　　　DO

Devil's Club ⅛　　　DO

Arctic Willow 2½x　　　DO

Blue Clematis ¾x　　　DO

Big Sagebrush
Composite Family
Artemisia tridentata

This grayish-green shrub is easily recognized by the 3-cleft leaves and the aromatic sage odor. In the parks this shrub may vary from 1 to 4 feet high and have a definite trunk up to 2 inches in diameter. The yellowish flowers are borne in small heads and do not appear until late August or early September. Several species of this genus were used medicinally by Indians and white settlers. Tea made from the leaves was used in the treatment of sore eyes and colds. Many birds and mammals utilize this valuable wildlife food especially in combination with other browse and grasses. This species is found up the North Fork of the Flathead River near Polebridge and north to the Canadian line.

Rustyleaf Menziesia
Heath Family
Menziesia ferruginea

This thicket-forming shrub can reach 7 feet tall and has deciduous leaves that form rosettes at the end of slender, erect branches. The plants have a similar appearance to huckleberry plants especially in regard to the flower. The corolla of the flower is urn-shaped and is topped by 4 lobes. The 8 stamens have anthers opening by terminal pores. The fruits are dry capsules and are not edible. Additional names include fool's huckleberry and false azalea. This is a very widespread shrub in cool, moist coniferous forests.

Subalpine spiraea
Rose Family
Spiraea densiflora

The subalpine spiraea is quite distinctive and a much more attractive shrub than the white-flowered species *S. betulifolia*. Hiking the montane trails, the plant enthusiast will find this shrub on the moist slopes and beside fast moving streams up to 10,000 feet. Some can be found near Lunch Creek and along the Iceberg Lake Trail. It has a branched habit and grows to 3 feet in height. The rose-pink flowers are sweet-scented and are aggregated into flat-topped clusters about 1 or 2 inches across. The inflorescences are soft and fluffy in appearance due to many long, interlacing stamens of adjoining blossoms. The leaves are simple and bear small teeth on the margins. The generic name *Spiraea* comes from a Greek word meaning wreath.

Birchleaf Spiraea
Rose Family
Spiraea betulifolia

Spiraeas are familiar shrubs in our gardens and several wild species occur in North America. These plants are unique among members of the rose family in that they lack stipules at the base of the petioles. This particular species usually has a single erect stem between 1 and 3 feet high. The egg-shaped leaves are coarsely toothed toward the apex. The small but perfect flowers have 3 sepals, 5 petals and numerous stamens. There are usually 5 distinct pistils which develop into follicles which split down one side at maturity. Insects frequently cause galls to form in the flowers thus detracting from their beauty. This is one of the most common low shrubs of the two parks and is easily seen as one hikes the trails around the lakes. Blue grouse eat the leaves of this plant in the spring, and deer may feed on the tops in summer.

g Sagebrush ½x   RJS

Rustyleaf Menziesia 1x   DO

balpine Spiraea ¾x   DO

Birchleaf Spiraea ¾x   DO

Alpine Laurel
Heath Family

Kalmia microphylla

Alpine meadows or subalpine lake shores are the habitat for this small, straggling, evergreen shrub. The opposite leaves are leathery texture, and the margins are rolled under so that they appear narrowly linear. From the time flower buds appear until complete flower expansion occurs, the various changes are a delight to behold. At one stage the bud resembles a blob of cake frosting. The saucer-shaped flowers have 10 arched filaments bent under tension with each anther tucked into a pocket of the corolla; and when an insect visits a flower, the slightest touch of the anthers whips them forward to shower the insect's body with pollen. The visitor then flies to another flower and cross-pollination is assured.

Four-angled Mountain Heather
Heath Family

Cassiope tetragona

This circumboreal, dwarf shrub forms dense mats near timberline. The small scale-like leaves are 4-ranked, and each leaf has a prominent groove on the back. The white corolla is bell-shaped and nodding; there are 10 stamens. This species might be confused with another alpine species, *Phyllodoce glanduliflora*, (yellow mountain heather) except that the latter has an urn-shaped corolla and sticky, glandular hairs on the flower stalks. This species grows on moist, rocky bluffs and benches, especially in the Logan Pass area.

Pink Heather; Red Mountainheath
Heath Family

Phyllodoce empetriformis

This evergreen, mat-forming shrub produces flowers singly in the axils of leaves which are aggregated at or near the stem tips. Note how the flowers always nod and the stamens are well hidden within the 5-lobed corolla. This species and a similar species, *P. glanduliflora,* grow on wet sites at high altitudes often around the shores of subalpine lakes. Late July and August are the months in which to find the blossoms. Alpine laurel is often found growing with this plant.

Yellow Mountain Heather
Heath Family

Phyllodoce glanduliflora

These tiny alpine shrubs are a beautiful sight when they bloom on a rugged alpine slope. The height of the plant varies from 4 to 15 inches and the evergreen leaves appear as miniature fir needles. The urn-shaped flowers and the pedicels are covered with delicate, gland-tipped hairs. Note how the flowers always nod and the 7-10 stamens are well hidden within the corolla. The seed capsules are reddish colored in the fall. Look for this species on moist ledges in the Logan Pass area. When this species grows near *Phyllodoce empetriformis* they often hybridize to produce a plant with pale pink flowers.

ine Laurel   1½x   DO

Four-angled Mountain Heather   1¼x   DO

k Heather   1½x   DO

Yellow Mountain Heather   1½x   DO

Utah Honeysuckle

Honeysuckle Family

Lonicera utahensis

Known also as red twinberry, this shrub of mid to high elevations in the mountains varies from 2 to 5 feet high. In May and June the paired yellow flowers are a delight to behold. The 5 petals are united into a funnel-shaped tube which has a pronounced knob on one side which accumulates nectar. Nectar-robbing bees will visit the flowers and puncture the corolla swelling to suck out the sweet reward. The red fruits are attached to the axil of the leaf by short, ¾-inch pedicels. Flowers and fruits separate this species from the black twinberry because they lack the subtending involucral bracts. The fruits are eaten by some birds and mammals. This species was first described from specimens collected in Utah, hence, the specific name.

Mountain Alder

Birch Family

Alnus incana var. *occidentalis*

The alders are tall shrubs or small trees of up to 20 feet in height, and they are found along rivers and streams or in moist meadows. The alternate, egg-shaped leaves have a doubly-toothed leaf margin. The flowers appear early in the spring before the leaf buds open. The pistillate and staminate flowers arise in separate clusters called catkins. The individual blooms are minute and pollination is accomplished by the wind. Because of persistent, woody scales on the female catkin, the entire structure looks like a miniature pine cone. Some Indians used a tea made from the bark for the treatment of hemorrhoids. Beaver cut the stems of alders for building their dams and lodges as well as using the bark for food.

Utah Honeysuckle 1½x   RJS

Utah Honeysuckle 1x   RJS

Mountain Alder ¾   RJS

Black Twinberry;
Bearberry Honeysuckle Honeysuckle Family

Lonicera involucrata

This 3-6 foot shrub has a distinctive feature of an involucre of 2 bracts subtending the paired yellow flowers. There are no sepals, and the 5 petals are fused into a narrow tube. The stamens and nectaries are enclosed within the tube of the corolla. Following the June flowers, the fruits begin their development and by late August these berries are juicy and purple-black in appearance. The persistent involucral bracts become dark red and expand backward to further expose the berries. The fruits are reported to be mildly poisonous, but the taste is so unpleasant that they are seldom eaten by people. They are eaten, however, by birds and animals. Black twinberry grows only where soil moisture is abundant. Blooming occurs early in May in the North Fork.

Redosier Dogwood Dogwood Family

Cornus stolonifera

The red bark of the slender twigs of this rather variable shrub makes the best field identification character. Combine this with the flat-topped clusters of flowers in the spring and white berries (a 2-seeded drupe) in the fall and it becomes the easiest shrub to recognize along streams and rivers. The opposite leaves are lanceolate and in September take on brilliant colors. Like other members of the family, this species bears flowers which are constructed on a plan of 4 — 4 sepals, 4 petals and 4 stamens. Seeds of the white to bluish fruits provide winter food for birds and mammals. The name *osier* refers to a pliable branch used in basket weaving, hence the name, redosier.

Black Twinberry   1x   DO

Black Twinberry   ¾x   RJS

Redosier Dogwood   ¾x   RJS

Redosier Dogwood   ¾x   RJS

Thimbleberry

Rubus parviflorus

Thimbleberry belongs in the same genus as raspberries and blackberries, but can be readily separated from these two latter shrubs by the undivided, simple leaves and the thornless stems. This wide-spreading shrub may reach from 3 to 6 feet high and is quite common at low to middle altitudes in wooden areas. The large, white flowers (often 2 inches across) have a cylindric receptacle which is covered with numerous pistils. Following pollination and fertilization, this aggregation of pistils forms the bright red, raspberry-like fruit. The August ripening berries, which are quite tart, are relished by many animals, from small birds to grizzly bears. This attractive shrub with maple-like leaves is especially prevalent in the northern Rockies where it thrives in consistent pathways of avalanches.

Bog or Dwarf Birch

Birch Family

Betula glandulosa

Like the mountain alder, the flowers of this species are small, inconspicuous and borne in slender catkins. The flowers are fully developed as the leaves begin to appear. Such early flowering in the spring favors wind pollination. Both male and female catkins develop on the same tree. Birches are best known for their paper-like bark which peels off in thin, papery layers. Grouse feed on the catkins and fruit. Moose and beaver are reported to feed on the young resinous twigs. This shrubby species is found along streams and on other wet sites, especially near timberline.

Thimbleberry 1x   RJS

Thimbleberry ¾x   RJS

Bog Birch ¾x   RJS

Common Snowberry

Symphoricarpos albus

The common snowberry is a 3-6 foot shrub with numerous slender twigs, and it is one of the few woody species with large white berries. The simple leaves are opposite and oval in outline. The flowers are bell-shaped, arranged in dense terminal clusters. If the corolla tube is slit lengthwise, white hairs are revealed on the inner face of the 5 lobes. This feature, plus its hollow stems, is significant in separating this species from related species. Snowberries are an important wildlife food in western parks. The non-poisonous berries ripen in late August and remain on the bushes even after they freeze. These 2-seeded berries are especially valuable as food for grouse and songbirds. An extract of the stems was used by the Indians for the treatment of stomach problems. Many people report that the odor from the flowers is unpleasant.

Swamp Gooseberry

Currant Family

Ribes lacustre

This low, bristly shrub grows to 3-4 feet high and is found in moist woods and stream banks up to subalpine areas. The stem is prickly and has sharp spines at the nodes. The flower parts are borne along the margins of a saucer-shaped hypanthium. The sepals are the most obvious part of a newly opened flower. The tiny, red petals are smaller and alternate with the sepals. The berries are purple-black and have some surface hairs. Despite the glandular hairs, the fruit is palatable. Other species of this genus which are spineless are called currants. This genus is the alternate host to the white pine blister rust which was introduced from Europe. Dead branches and tops of gooseberry are symptoms of disease caused by this rust which also attacks whitebark pine.

Mockorange; Syringa

Hydrangea Family

Philadelphus lewisii

At one time this medium-sized shrub was classified in the same genus as lilac, *Syringia*. That generic name is now retained as one of the common names. This shrub is important as the state flower of Idaho. Each flower has 4 petals enclosing about 30 yellow stamens and a single pistil. The fruit is a woody capsule. Mockorange is found on rocky hillsides of sagebrush deserts to ponderosa pine and Douglas-fir forests. While not a preferred food, it will be browsed by deer and elk. The specific name honors Captain Meriweather Lewis who collected the plant in Idaho. This sweet smelling shrub can be seen in McDonald Valley and on the Kintla drainage.

Common Snowberry 1x   DO

Common Snowberry 1x   DO

Swamp Gooseberry 1x   DO

Mockorange 1x   DO

Alpine Wintergreen

Heath Family

Gaultheria humifusa

This sprawling, evergreen shrub is often overlooked and ignored until the fruits ripen in late August. The alternate leaves are only ½ inch long, with margins nearly entire. The white flowers are urn-shaped and vary between ⅛ to ½ inch long. The calyx is glabrous. The red berries and young leaves are edible for man, grouse and deer. The leaves of all *Gaultheria* species yield an oil on steam distillation that has been considered an antirheumatic. This oil of wintergreen, or methyl salicylate, was formerly used as a folk remedy for body aches and pains. Look for these plants in moist soil near bogs and alpine lakes.

Cascade Mountain Ash

Rose Family

Sorbus scopulina

Cascade mountain ash is one of the most attractive shrubs of the rose family. The flat-topped flower clusters are 3 to 6 inches across. The compound leaves are alternate and each one is composed of 5 to 13 leaflets having finely toothed margins. The brilliant red-orange fruits mature by late August and although they are bitter to human taste, they are useful to wildlife. Birds, especially grosbeaks and grouse, and bears are regular feeders on the fruits. This shrub is found at all elevations, and it is often abundant on burned over forest land and snowslides. Look for the colorful fruits along Going to the Sun Highway. One other shrubby species of *Sorbus* occurs in the parks — Sitka mountain ash *(Sorbus sitchensis)*. Its leaflets are rounded at the tip and the fruits are red. Flower occurs in June and early July.

Alpine Wintergreen   1x   RJS

Cascade Mountain Ash   ¾x   RJS

Cascade Mountain Ash ¾x   RJS

Black Hawthorn
Rose Family
Crataegus douglasii

Hundreds of names have been proposed for the many species of hawthorn, and as a group they are perhaps the most difficult to classify in the rose family. The generic name, *Crataegus,* is a Greek word meaning strong, in reference to its tough wood. The genus can be readily distinguished even in the winter because no other rosaceous tree or shrub has the long and simple thorns (up to one inch in length). The white, ill-smelling flowers are borne in clusters at the ends of the branches. By late August the small apple-like fruits have reached maturity and provide food for many birds and small animals. The Indians of some regions used to gather the fruits or "haws" and dry them for winter use. The thorny branches of this shrub provide good cover for small birds and mammals.

Grouse Whortleberry
Heath Family
Vaccinium scoparium

This low shrub seldom grows more than 12 inches high and is a characteristic ground cover of cool, moderately dry coniferous forests. The broom-like branches are green and covered with oval-shaped leaves up to ½ inch in length. The urn-shaped flowers hang downward and are pale pink in color. The juicy, red berries are attractive to many birds and animals, including man. While the fruit of this species is sweet and high in flavor, it takes hours to pick enough for a batch of jam. Two other low shrub *Vacciniums* are found in this area: *V. caespitosum,* dwarf huckleberry, which can be identified by its stems that are round in cross-section, and *V. myrtillus,* dwarf bilberry, which typically does not have broom-like branches.

Mountain Lover; Myrtle Pachistima
Staff-tree Family
Pachistima myrsinites

This evergreen shrub has the appearance of low growing boxwood and grows in a wide range of environments. The opposite leaves have serrate leaf margins. The diminutive flowers are red, saucer-shaped and constructed on a plan of 4. One can remember the scientific name of this species by repeating the simple saying, "Pa kissed ma for mercenary reasons." Wildlife, such as elk and deer, have been observed eating the plant. Flowers occur in June. It has been found as high as the Garden Wall Trail.

Black Hawthorn ¾x   RJS

Black Hawthorn 1x   RJS

Grouse Whortleberry 1½x   DO

Mountain Lover 1x   DO

Wild Rose; Woods Rose

Rose Family

Rosa woodsii

Because of their wide distribution and fragrant flowers, the wild rose is perhaps the most quickly recognized of all the flowering shrubs. The showy flowers, in addition to numerous stamens, have several pistils which are enclosed by the cup-like receptacles. After the petals fall, this entire sructure becomes an aggregate fruit (called a rose hip) of great importance to wildlife. The vitamin-rich hips remain on the shrubs throughout the winter, supplying food for many birds and mammals. This shrub is also browsed by big game animals and live-stock. The Indians gathered the fruits for food and used the roots for treatments of ailments. Harrington suggests many uses of rose hips and emphasizes the variability of the fruits. There are at least 4 other species of *Rosa* in the two parks. The prickly rose, *R. acicularis,* is the floral emblem of Alberta and the Arkansas rose, *R. arkansana,* is the state flower of North Dakota.

Alder Buckthorn

Buckthorn Family

Rhamnus alnifolia

This is a low, spreading shrub which is readily distinguishable in summer by its finely toothed leaves, and in winter by its scaly buds but no thorns. Each leaf has 6 to 8 prominent veins. The small axillary flowers are greenish-yellow and the petals are generally absent. The berry-like fruit becomes blackish and contains 2 to 3 small nutlets. This plant resembles black twinberry in general appearance but the latter has opposite instead of alternate twigs. Both can be found on the same site. The closely related tree of the Pacific Northwest, *Rhamnus purshiana*, cascara, was utilized medicinally by several Indian tribes. They boiled the bark to prepare a laxative syrup. Alder buckthorn likewise has bark containing the laxative. It is found in moist bottom lands, along rivers and streams, and it is common at Goathaunt Ranger Station. Bears have been seen eating the berries.

Wild Rose   1x   RJS

Wild Rose   1x   RJS

Alder Buckthorn   ¾x   RJS

Canadian Buffaloberry; Soapberry
Oleaster Family

Shepherdia canadensis

This unarmed shrub is often found in the shade of the coniferous woods, sometimes even approaching timberline, but is more commonly found at lower elevations. The flowers appear in June and are inconspicuous as the petals are missing. The upper surface of the leaves is dull green, while the lower surface is silver, attractively spotted with brown dots. The intriguing red-orange berries brighten the branches by mid-August, but do not be misled into eating the fruit as it is bitter and astringent, and the taste lingers on for hours. Birds and bears, however, find the berries good eating. *Shepherdia agrentea,* thorny buffaloberry, is a related species found in coulees and river valleys of the prairie region of southern Alberta and Montana. The raw berries have a sharp, sour taste, but they can be made into a delicious jelly.

Shrubby Cinquefoil
Rose Family

Potentilla fruiticosa

Beginning in June and extending into September, this shrub has one of the longest blooming periods of any species in the parks. Since the flower has 5 petals, 5 sepals and numerous stamens, it is very much like a wild rose, but the plant is always thornless. The leafy stems are erect or ascending and grow to 4 feet in height. The generic name, *Potentilla,* is from the Latin word *poten* referring to the powerful medicinal value of some species. The species name, *fruticosa,* means shrubby. This shrub is worthy of cultivation and many horticultural varieties are available through nurserymen. Wild animals will browse this shrub especially in winter, and to the trained observer this species can serve as an indicator of plant overgrazing. This species grows on grasslands near St. Mary and at timberline on Logan Pass.

Labrador Tea; Trapper's Tea
Heath Family

Ledum glandulosum

This evergreen shrub reaches a height of about 30 inches. The oval to oblong leaves are fragrant when crushed, and there is a tendency for the leaf margins to curl under. The white flowers are about ½ inch across, and the regular corolla is composed of 5 spreading petals and a variable number of stamens (8-12) considerably longer than the style. The fruiting capsules are brown and split into 5 sections. A similar eastern species was used as a substitute for tea, the use of which is responsible for the common name. Flowering occurs from late June to August. This is not a common species in the northern Rocky Mountains. A few specimens are growing near the headquarters of G.N.P.

Canadian Buffaloberry ¾x   RJS

Shrubby Cinquefoil   1x   RJS

Labrador Tea   ¾x   RJS

Whiplash Willow

Willow Family

Salix lasiandra

As a group, the willows are easily recognized by their characteristic branches and catkins, yet it is often difficult to distinguish between many of the species. The whiplash willow is a spreading shrub 3 to 15 feet high. The flowers are unisexual; the staminate and pistillate flowers are both arranged in catkins but on different plants. The pistillate catkin in this species is up to 2½ inches in length, and by the time the fruits open, the numerous seeds are hairy. The buds and small, tender portions of the twigs are staple food for several species of grouse. The foliage and twigs furnish browse for moose, elk and deer. The bark is one of the favorite foods of the beaver.

Red Raspberry

Rose Family

Rubus idaeus

This native red raspberry looks very much like a cultivated raspberry though the small fruits are somewhat crumbly. It is commonly found above 6,000 feet on rocky talus slops. The plant has compound leaves with 3 to 5 leaflets, and the erect stems are prickly. The white flowers are ½ to ¾ inch across and continue to appear until mid-August. The red berries which ripen from late July to September are sweet and edible and are a favorite of many birds and mammals. The genus *Rubus* is a critical and difficult genus because the species are interfertile and often apomictic (able to produce seed without pollination). Look for this shrub in the North Fork area and in avalanche runs in Belly River and Waterton Valley.

White Virginsbower

Buttercup Family

Clematis ligusticifolia

This semi-woody, climbing vine has staminate and pistillate flowers on separate plants. The clusters of small flowers have no petals, but have 4-5 showy sepals. Later in the season the persistent styles of the achenes become long and feathery, enabling the fruits to be dispersed far and wide. The vines climb by coiling the leaf stalks about stems of shrubs and trees. Some Indian tribes used an infusion of this plant for skin ailments such as eczema. This species is easily separated from the related vine, *C. columbiana,* by the cluster small white flowers.

Whiplash Willow ¾x

Red Raspberry ⅔x

White Virginsbower 1x

Elderberry

Sambucus racemosa

This is a circumboreal shrub that inhabits woods and streambanks. The small, numerous flowers are white to cream in color and arranged in flat-topped, compound clusters. By mid-August the solitary pistils form the fruits. As these fruits get heavy, the erect inflorescences hang downward. Wherever this shrub grows, the berries have been used for making jelly, pies and wine. The roots, bark and mature leaves are considered poisonous to livestock, so use should be limited to fruits and flowers. Moose, deer and elk, however, will browse this shrub heavily. Several varieties have been described, but all elderberries are characterized by pithy stems, opposite compound leaves and red to black berries. Berries should not be eaten until fully ripe.

Low Oregon Grape

Berberis repens

This creeping, dwarf shrub forms a portion of the ground cover in sagebrush and aspen to spruce-fir communities. Every spring dense clusters of yellow flowers brighten the appearance of the pinnately compound leaves. Each leaflet is prickly toothed, similar to the leaves of a holly plant. Usually each flower has 6 sepals, 6 petals and 6 stamens. By August the plants have produced rather sparse clusters of grape-like berries. Along with the ripening of the fruit, some leaves turn beautiful shades of red or purple. Some people describe the berries as having a bitter taste, but a number of authors recommend using them in making jelly, jam and wine. The fruits are sometimes penetrated by grubs, rendering them inedible, and some plants may go for years without producing a good berry crop.

Elderberry ¾x   RJS

Elderberry ¾x   RJS

Low Oregon Grape 1½x   RJS

Low Oregon Grape ¾x   RJS

Globe Huckleberry

Heath Family

Vaccinium globulare

Other common names for this widespread shrub include blueberry, bilberry and whortleberry, and this abundance of names is an indication of the fact that many species have long been used in the English-speaking world. The plant varies from 2 to 4 feet in height, and it is very popular with park visitors because of its sweet, juicy berries. The globe-shaped flowers are greenish-white or pinkish. The 5 petals are united into a tube and bear 10 stamens on the inner surface. The leaves are quite variable in shape. By mid-August the wine-red to purple-black berries begin to appear, and there is considerable competition between birds, bears and man for perhaps the most tasty fruit of the parks. Deer, moose and elk browse freely on the stems and leaves.

Mountainspray; Creambush

Rose Family

Holodiscus discolor

This hillside shrub varies from 3 to 5 feet in height and produces flowers arranged in pyramid-like, loose clusters. The individual creamy-white flowers have 5 petals, generally 20 stamens and 5 pistils. The small, dry, flattened fruits were eaten by the Indians. The alternate leaves are toothed to shallowly lobed and have a silvery-gray surface underneath. A similar shrub, ninebark, might be confused with mountainspray except that the bark of the two shrubs is quite different. Ninebark has loose and peeling bark, whereas mountainspray has ribbed branches and twigs. The dried flowers usually persist into the following growing season. Look for this shrub along the highway near St. Mary Lake and near the goat lick on Highway 2 east of Essex.

Rocky Mountain Maple

Maple Family

Acer glabrum var. *glabrum*

This species of maple is a shrub or small tree from 12 to 30 feet high and has an uneven-topped crown. The 3-5-lobed leaves vary from 2 to 3 inches across and are supported by reddish, slender petioles. Greenish-yellow flowers appear with the unfolding leaves in loose, drooping clusters. The colorful double-winged fruits mature by mid-August; the swollen seed portion is strongly wrinkled and indented. The wings of the fruit are at a very narrow angle or almost parallel. Many horticulturists recommend this maple as suitable for use as an ornamental in gardens because of its diminutive size and attractive fall coloration. This is one of the first shrubs to turn color in the late summer. Deer, elk and moose feed on the leaves and twigs.

Globe Huckleberry   1¼x   DO

Mountainspray   ⅛x   GNP

Rocky Mountain Maple   ⅞x   RJS

Silverberry

Elaeagnus commutata

Flowers and fruits of this shrub are not conspicuous, but the silvery pubescence which covers the leaves makes this species unique and easy to recognize. Each fragrant flower has a tubular shape and is silvery on the outside and yellowish on the inside. There are 4 small stamens that alternate with the perianth lobes. Note how the remains of the flower hang on to the ends of the ½-inch-long silvery fruit. While the fruit looks like a berry, it is really quite hard and bony and is surrounded by the soft, mealy calyx. This 4-6 foot shrub grows on sandy stream banks or lake shores on the east side of G.N.P. and along the North Fork Flathead River. The fruits, which persist through winter, may be eaten raw or cooked.

Common Chokecherry

Rose Family

Prunus virginiana var. *melanocarpa*

The common chokecherry is a large shrub up to 20 feet in height and is known to many westerners as a source of small, tart cherries. The 5-petaled white flowers are about ⅓ of an inch across and are borne in attractive cylindrical clusters of 3 to 4 inches long. The fruits, which gradually become bright red and finally almost black, ripen during August or early September. While tempting to the eye, the fruit is disappointing because it is harshly astringent to the taste and is nearly all stone. Many songbirds and mammals, however, relish the cherries and aid in the dispersal of seeds. The fruits were very popular with the Indians; they would grind up the fruit, stones and all, dry the material in the sun, and store for later use. They also mixed this dried fruit with dried meat and fat to produce the famous concentrated food, pemmican. Chokecherries are suitable for making delicious jelly, and the bark has been used to make a substitute for tea. The bitter cherry, *Prunus emarginata,* can be found along the trail to Iceberg Lake. The flowers of this species are fewer in number and are arranged in an umbellate inflorescence. This shrub is especially common in transition areas in W.N.P.

Deerbrush; Snowbrush Ceanothus

Buckthorn Family

Ceanothus velutinus

In California the species of *Ceanothus* are numerous and confusing, yet in G.N.P. there are only two species. The second species, *C. sanguineus,* is called the redstem ceanothus. Usually *C. velutinus* is a rather low rounded shrub 2 to 5 feet high. Another common name, varnish bush, comes from the shiny or somewhat sticky coating on the upper surface of the egg-shaped, leathery leaves. The small, white flowers are borne in showy clusters, and a close look at one flower will reveal the 5 petals have a scoop-like shape. A soapy lather may be obtained by rubbing a few flower clusters between the hands with a small amount of water. Because the leaves are not deciduous, deer, elk and moose browse the herbage and birds eat the seeds. The seeds of both species can lie dormant and viable for many years and germinate after a fire.

ilverberry 1x   RJS

Silverberry ¾x   RJS

ommon Chokecherry ¾   DO

Deerbrush ¾x   RJS

Poison Ivy

Rhus radicans

The plant is a sub-erect shrub or woody-stemmed vine which is variable in habit of growth. The best identifying feature is the presence of the shiny, 3-foliate leaves, mostly oval to lanceolate with entire margins. The small, greenish-white flowers give rise to dull, yellowish waxy fruits, ¼ inch in diameter. Poison ivy contains a substance chemically similar to lacquer. This resin is non-volatile and cannot produce dermatitis unless a person actually contacts the active compound. The allergen may be carried to the person on particles of carbon in smoke, or by pets, clothing or tools. The resin clings to the skin and may be removed by washing with a strong soap 5 to 10 minutes after contact. Certain ointments may relieve itching. The Indians of southern California applied a mash of poison ivy leaves to cure ringworm. This species is a recent invader of disturbed sites, particularly on the Middle Fork.

Sitka Mountain Ash

Sorbus sitchensis

This variable shrub of the rose family is common throughout the Pacific Northwest, but grows best above 3,000 feet in the mountains. The leaves are pinnately compound and have 7-11 leaflets. Each leaflet has a blunt (subacute) tip with serrations limited to the upper half. Young twigs and buds are covered with a rufous pubescence. The white flowers are grouped into flat clusters, usually 2-3 inches across. The fleshy, pomaceous fruits are unmatched in brilliance and beauty and are eagerly sought by migrating birds. Deer keep this 5-8 foot bush well trimmed. The most useful feature in separating this species from *Sorbus scopulina* is the leaflet. In the case of *S. scopulina* the leaflets are slimmer and sharply pointed with serrations the full length of the margins.

Poison Ivy *3x* RJS

Poison Ivy ½x RJS

Sitka Mountain Ash 1x DO

Common Timothy
Grass Family
Phleum pratense
This tufted perennial may reach 3 feet tall, the stems usually becoming enlarged and more or less bulbous at the base. The photograph reveals the slender flowering head at its most beautiful period. Each floret has 3 stamens and in a matter of a few hours, the filaments elongate enough so that the delicate anthers are exposed for wind pollination. This species of grass is native to Europe and has repeatedly escaped cultivation to become established in most areas. It is abundant in the Belly River Valley and in the grasslands on both sides of the Continental Divide. A native species, *P. alpinum,* is found along streambanks and meadows in the mountains.

Yellow Coralroot; Northern Coralroot
Orchid Family
Corallorhiza trifida
This is the smallest species of coralroots and is often undetected in the deep shade of the coniferous forest. It is also the most common Canadian species of *Corallorhiza*. The golden yellow or greenish-yellow stems accentuated by the white lips of the flowers give the plant a ghostly appearance. The specific name, *trifida,* comes from the Latin meaning split into three parts and refers to the three lobes of the lip. The sometimes greenish-colored stem would seem to imply that the plant may be able to manufacture some of its carbohydrates. Most species of coralroots, however, live as parasites on soil fungi. Look for this plant in North Fork Valleys.

Stinging Nettle
Nettle Family
Urtica dioica
Stinging nettle plants are perennials with creeping rootstocks and reach a stem height of up to 6 feet. The stiff, stinging hairs on the stems and branches are filled with a skin-irritating acid which will cause a burning sensation for many minutes. In spite of the stinging hairs, the plant has always been popular as a food, especially as a pot herb, cooked and used like spinach. The stinging principle is inactivated by cooking. The small, greenish flowers are arranged in dangling spikes. Watch for the plants along streams, canyons, moist trailsides, and in disturbed areas.

False Hellebore
Lily Family
Veratrum viride
In the springtime the plant sends up fleshy shoots wrapped in distinctive leaves which are strongly veined and pleated. Later in the season the flowering shoots may reach 5 feet. False hellebore grows in wet meadows at middle elevations to timberline. The individual flowers have similar perianth segments and 6 yellow stamens. The plant contains poisonous alkaloids and is especially toxic in the early spring to grazing mammals, particularly sheep. If ewes graze this plant during pregnancy, they give birth to deformed lambs. Some of these plants can be found near Lunch Creek, the first drainage east of Logan Pass. It is also common on the west side of Boulder Pass.

Common Timothy   1x   RK

Yellow Coralroot   1x   DO

Stinging Nettle   ⅛x   RJS

False Hellebore   ⅛x   RJS

Crested Wheatgrass

Grass Family

Agropyron cristatum

This tufted perennial grows from 20-40 inches tall, and like many other grasses has a flattened, spike-like inflorescence. Individual florets have small, green bracts and 3 stamens. Pollination is accomplished by the wind. Crested wheatgrass has been widely introduced from Eurasia to revegetate our semi-arid rangelands and dry pastures, and as a result has become well established in several parks. The value of grasses as a source of food for man and herbivores cannot be overemphasized. Bluebunch wheatgrass, *A. spicatum,* is a native species that is common throughout the Northwest.

Showy Green Gentian

Gentian Family

Frasera speciosa

The showy green gentian, one of the tallest of the herbaceous plants, has a thick stem with a curious mixture of numerous leaves and green flower whorls. Each individual flower has a plan of 4 sepals, 4 petals and 4 stamens. Many insects are attracted to the rather elaborate nectar glands and purple spots on each petal. While the plant is perennial, it flowers only once and then dies. It is found in open or wooded foothills to subalpine slopes. The fruits are rather prominent capsules that produce copious amounts of seed.

Dwarf Mistletoe

Dwarf Mistletoe Family

Arceuthobium americanum

The dwarf mistletoes are extremely specialized and reduced plants. Almost every conifer species has its own distinctive species or race of *Arceuthobium*. These parasites have a long period of coexistence with their host and seldom kill a tree. Dwarf mistletoes have specialized penetrating roots (haustoria), stems with swollen nodes and opposite scalelike leaves. The flowers are unisexual and inconspicuous. The seeds are explosively shot from the fruit for distances up to 45 feet. The sticky seeds eventually germinate on the branches of the host. Sometimes the penetrating haustoria cause the branches to expand to nearly twice the normal diameter. This species is very specific in parasitizing only the lodgepole pine. Some squirrels have been observed feeding on the mistletoes during the winter.

Crested Wheatgrass ¾x

Showy Green Gentian   1x

Dwarf Mistletoe   1x

Western False Solomon's Seal

Lily Family

Smilacina racemosa

The erect or arching stems of this perennial herb arise from branching underground stems and may reach 2½ feet tall. The broad ovate leaves lack a petiole and tend to sheathe the stem. The numerous flowers are in a branched raceme. Like many others in the lily family, the perianth consists of 6 equal segments. This plant is quite similar to star solomon's seal, *Smilacina stellata,* but the latter species has an unbranched raceme and relatively few flowers. Bright red berries develop later in the season and were eaten by the Indians of British Columbia. Flowering occurs from late May through July.

Common Beargrass

Lily Family

Xerophyllum tenax

This species is very striking when it covers an open slope with flowering stems up to 5 feet tall. The base of the plant has a mass of wiry, grasslike leaves. The edges of the leaves are rough to the touch because of short stiff hairs. The flowers are borne in a dense raceme which may be 6 to 8 inches long. The clumps of leaves arise from a thick rhizome, and any particular offshoot may not flower for several years. Ultimately an erect flowering stalk will arise and die down after fruiting. The mountain goat will eat the leaves, and elk and bighorn sheep eat the blossoms. This species is common on coarse textured soils near the park entrance at West Glacier and extends to timberline.

Mountain Death Camas

Lily Family

Zigadenus elegans

All members of this genus should be treated as poisonous even though they vary in their toxicity. The alkaloids present are poisonous to man and livestock. The species pictured is the most widespread and certainly the most attractive. The flowers are ½ to ¾ inch broad and both sepals and petals have yellow-green glands near the base. The plants are 1 to 2 feet tall and have folded grasslike leaves which arise from bulbs situated 3 to 6 inches below the ground surface. The bulbs have been confused with mariposa lily and wild onion. This species grows in alpine and high mountain meadows.

Meadow Death Camas

Lily Family

Zigadenus venenosus

Death camas is the common name for several species of this genus that are poisonous to livestock and man. Toxic alkaloids are mainly concentrated in the bulb, but children have been poisoned by eating the flowers. Bulbs of this species were occasionally confused with blue camas by Indians and early settlers, often causing disastrous results. The stem of this perennial reaches from 1 to 2 feet tall when in full flower. The individual blossoms are about ¼ inch wide and have the typical lily flower constructed on a plan of three. In both parks look for the flowers in June and July in sagebrush communities.

Western False Solomon's Seal ¾x   DO

Beargrass 1x   DO

Mountain Death Camas 1x   DO

Meadow Death Camas 1x   DO

Miner's Lettuce

Purslane Family

Montia perfoliata

This succulent annual bears two kinds of leaves making it easy to recognize. The basal leaves have long petioles and a variable broad blade. The upper leaves are like shallow cups being formed by 2 opposite leaves joined around the stem. The white to pink flowers have a variable number of petals and stamens, 2 to 5. The Indians and early settlers used the young plants in the spring as a salad. The shoots and leaves were also cooked as "greens." The sprawling stamens are about 2 to 6 inches long and favor moist banks and slopes, often in shade.

Beaked Sedge

Sedge Family

Carex rostrata

The inclusion of only one species of *Carex* in this book does not do justice to this very important genus. More than 1,000 species occur in all parts of the world, and more than 100 species are found in a variety of habitats of the Rocky Mountains. The flowers are unisexual, and since they are dependent on wind pollination, they lack any perianth members. Vegetatively, sedges can be distinguished from grasses by their leaves arranged in 3 rows or ranks around a triangular solid stem. In grasses the leaves are 2-ranked encircling a round hollow stem. *Carex geyeri* grows in the shade of lodgepole pine and provides food for elk, mountain sheep and deer. The species illustrated is common in drying ponds.

Wild Buckwheat

Buckwheat Family

Eriogonum umbellatum

Also known as sulphurflower, this plant is especially showy from sagebrush plains to mountain ridges. The sulphur-yellow blossoms are in an umbrella-like cluster at the top of a 10 to 12-inch flowering stalk, while the numerous leaves grow very near to the ground and accumulate bits of organic matter to enrich the soil. Each flower of an umbel-like cluster has 6 perianth parts which cannot be separated into sepals or petals. A related species, *E. ovalifolium,* is widely distributed and extends upward even above timberline where it becomes dwarfed and mat-like. The best recognition feature of *E. ovalifolium* is a lack of any leaves and bracts on the stem. The genus *Eriognum* is difficult and has about 300 species, mostly in the western United States.

Miner's Lettuce   1x

Beaked Sedge   1x

Wild Buckwheat   1x

Bare-stemmed Mitrewort

Saxifrage Family

Mitella nuda

The flowers of mitreworts are famous for their delicate petals which are cut or divided into narrow lobes or segments. Viewed under a hand lens, they appear to have been crafted by a master jeweler. Mitreworts are often overlooked because their blossoms are so small. The species illustrated has 10 stamens and pointed calyx lobes. The leaves are roundish and have a toothed margin. The flower stems stand from 10-18 inches above the basal leaves. A closely related species, *M. pentandra,* alpine mitrewort, has only 5 stamens opposite the petals. *M. breweri,* Brewer's mitrewort, with 5 stamens opposite the sepals, is also found in the parks.

Pointed Mariposa

Lily Family

Calochortus apiculatus

The genus, *Calochortus,* is one of the most beautiful in the lily family. It is readily recognized by the narrow sepals in contrast to the broad, conspicuously marked petals. Boiled bulbs have the flavor of potatoes and were eaten by the Indians and early settlers when food was scarce. The pointed mariposa can be distinguished by the small, dark spot in the middle of each petal. Several species thrive in many western states, but cities and towns encroaching upon the habitat have left some species in a precarious position. Grasslands, foothills and open forests are the habitats for this species.

Claspleaf Twisted-stalk

Lily Family

Streptopus amplexifolius

The flowers of this perennial herb are axillary, dangling at the ends of slender peduncles. The generic name, *Streptopus,* means twisted foot in reference to the bent or twisted flower stalks. The specific name, *amplexifolius,* means clasping-leaf in reference to the sessile leaves. This 2-4-foot plant grows only where the soil is wet along streams in the canyons. By August the greenish-white flowers have given way to bright red, oval berries about ½ inch long. The juicy berries may be eaten raw or cooked in stews or soup.

Baneberry

Buttercup Family

Actaea rubra

In the shade of very moist conferous forests this herbaceous plant reaches 2 to 3 feet high. The compound leaves are thin and delicate, and the ultimate segments are deeply sawtoothed. The elongated flower cluster is 3 to 7 inches in length and consists of many small flowers, each with 5 to 10 fragile, white petals. There are two color phases of the fruits — bright scarlet and china white — prompting some botanists to classify these as separate varieties. Hardin and Arena (1969) in their book, *Human Poisoning from Native and Cultivated Plants,* suggest that all parts of the plant, particularly the berries, contain a poisonous glucoside which causes acute stomach cramps, vomiting, etc. This species is well distributed in both the parks and is common in Belly River Valley.

Bare-stemmed Mitrewort 1x DO

Pointed Mariposa ¾x DO

Claspleaf Twisted-stalk ¾x RJS

Baneberry 1x RJS

Ladies-tresses; Pearl Twist
Orchid Family
Spiranthes romanzoffiana
The creamy white flowers of this plant are best appreciated with the aid of a hand lens. Like other orchid flowers, there are 3 sepals, 3 petals, and the stamens and pistil are combined into one unit. The flower spike is crowded and so tightly spiraled as to produce 3 vertical rows of overlapping white flowers. Check the delicate flowers for fragrance. Look particularly for the plant in Kishenehn Valley of the North Fork.

Western Rattlesnake Plantain
Orchid Family
Goodyera oblongifolia
The word, plantain, has been applied to many unrelated species of plants and comes from the Latin word *planta* meaning the sole of the foot. In the case of this orchid it refers to the broad, flat, evergreen leaves. The adjective, rattlesnake, refers to the reticulated, light markings on the leaves, which reminded the early settlers of the patterns on snakes. This species has a horizontal creeping rhizome, and at its end it produces a rosette of leaves, each leaf bearing a prominent central stripe. The inflorescence is one-sided and may bear up to 30 flowers. The flowering stem emerges from the center of the rosette and may reach a height of 18 inches or more. Flowering occurs from late July into September.

Alpine Lousewort
Figwort Family
Pedicularis contorta
Members of this genus have evolved a startling array of flower colors and forms to produce some very complex pollinator relationships. Furthermore, many species are semi-parasitic on the roots of other plants. The alpine lousewort has many basal leaves divided into narrow, toothed segments. The flowering racemes may elongate up to 12 inches. The corolla of the flower is bilabiate, the upper part forming a beak which is bent sideways and downward. This twisting of the corolla is reflected in the species name, *contorta*. This species is found on open slopes and drier meadows in the alpine region.

Northwest Twayblade
Orchid Family
Listera caurina
Extremely delicate and often overlooked, this species is uncommon in the wet coniferous forest. It can be separated from other green orchids by the broad, opposite leaves about midway on the stem and a loose raceme of tiny flowers with widely spreading sepals and petals. The greenish lip is dilated at the apex. Behind that apex, 2 parallel dark green stripes run up to a pair of rounded swellings at the base of the lip. They are so small that a 10x hand lens is needed. From the swellings rise a pair of minute appendages which spread to either side of the column. Heart-leaved twayblade, *L. cordata,* which grows in a similar habitat, can be distinguished by the conspicuous splitting of the lip, more than half the length of the lip.

Ladies-tresses   1¼x   DO

Western Rattlesnake Plantain   ½x   DO

Alpine Lousewort   ½x   DO

Northwest Twayblade   ¾x   DO

Yampah

Perideridia gairdneri

The individual white flowers of yampah are constructed on a plan of 5, clustered in compound umbels, a feature common to all members of this family. This erect, slender herb grows from 1 to 3 feet tall. As an important food plant of the Indians and mountain men, it was recognized by its slender leaves and its 2 to 3 fleshy roots just below the ground level. When eaten raw, these roots have a sweet, nutty, parsnip-like flavor. They can also be boiled, roasted or dried. The Belly River Valley is a good place to observe this plant.

Canada Violet

Violet Family

Viola canadensis

Recognition of this rather tall perennial violet is relatively easy because of the white flowers and leaf blades which are often wider than long and broadly heart-shaped. The lower petal of this bilaterally symmetrical flower has several distinctive purple lines that are called guide lines by students of pollination. There is good evidence that these lines direct insect visitors past the stamens to the sweet nectar. Harrington suggests that all species of violets are edible either raw in salads or cooked as pot herbs. The 300 or so species of violets are distributed on all continents of the earth except Antarctica. This plant grows only in cool, moist forests. Some can be found near the entrance to Avalanche Campground. It is also common in North Fork Valley where it blooms early in May.

Water Crowfoot

Buttercup Family

Ranunculus aquatilis

There are at least 12 species of buttercups in the two parks, and many of them offer some difficulty in identification. This aquatic species, however, is no problem because it is the only buttercup in the parks to have white flowers. This plant may have 2 kinds of leaves. The submerged leaves are divided into many thread-like branches, and floating leaves are broadly 3-5-lobed. Five thin sepals are quickly shed, and 5 unnotched petals are white with a yellow base. When not in flower, this plant could be mistaken for water milfoil, *Myriophyllum*. At times in late summer, shallow ponds and lake edges are literally covered with white blooms.

Yampah   1x   RJS

Canada Violet   ¾x   DO

Water Crowfoot   1x   RJS

White Trillium
Lily Family

Trillium ovatum

This perennial herb symbolizes the early spring arrival of the flowers and birds. It is found by streams and in open and dense woods from Alberta southward to Colorado. There is only one flower on the stem, and it is constructed on a plan of 3, with 3 sepals and 3 white petals turning rose with age. The generic name, *Trillium,* meaning three, makes reference to the most conspicuous characteristic of these plants, namely the 3 broad leaves below the single terminal flower. The fruits are berry-like capsules. Wake robin and birth root are other common names. This species is found in moist forest sites in McDonald Valley, and can be very abundant in some years (e.g. 1975) in North Fork.

Tofieldia; False Asphodel
Lily Family

Tofieldia glutinosa

This slender perennial, up to 16 inches high, has grass-like basal leaves. Wet, high mountain meadows and sandy soil around lakes or ponds provides the habitat requirements for this June, July and August bloomer. The sticky stem bears dense, terminal clusters of small, greenish-white flowers. The fruits of this species are more attractive than the flowers as they are plump and reddish-purple. In southern Europe the lileaceous genus, *Asphodel,* occurs; and, because of a superficial resemblance, *Tofieldia* has been called false asphodel.

Common Pearlyeverlasting
Composite Family

Anaphalis margaritacea

This widely distributed perennial occurs in clumps up to 2 feet tall, and it is covered with soft, woolly hairs especially on the lower surfaces of the lanceolate leaves. A good hand lens is needed to make out the details of the tiny flowers. Each flower-head has a pearly-white series of involucral bracts surrounding the tubular flowers. The bracts and flowers have the ability to retain their color and form for weeks — long after one would expect the blossoms to fall off. Thus the popular name is appropriate and descriptive. The specific name, *margaritacea,* is from a Greek word for pearl. The plants do not usually bloom until July.

Queencup; Beadlily
Lily Family

Clintonia uniflora

The delicate member of the lily family grows from underground rhizomes which inhabit moist soil in the shade of the coniferous forest. The white bell-shaped flowers consist of 6 similar petal-like segments, 6 stamens and a 3-lobed stigma. The 2-3 basal leaves are oblong and 4 to 6 inches long. The fruit is a blue berry which is non-edible. The combination of rhizomes, broad leaves and white flowers set this one species and genus apart from all other lily genera. The leaves of this plant can be mistaken for those of glacier lilies.

White Trillium 1x   DO

Tofieldia 1x   RJS

Pearlyeverlasting 1x   DO

Queencup 1x   DO

Sickletop Lousewort; Parrots-beak
Figwort Family
Pedicularis racemosa
The white flowers of parrots-beak distinguish it from the other two common species of this genus, the bracted lousewort and elephanthead. The curving and flattening of the 2 upper petals are responsible for the common name. The united, upper petals enclose the anthers and taper into a slender, downcurved beak almost touching the prominent lower lip. This species is unique in the genus in having undivided leaves scattered along the stem. Flowering time varies from late June to August. The generic name, *Pedicularis,* is derived from the Latin word meaning louse and relates to an ancient superstition that the use of plants of this genus for livestock food caused louse infestation.

Western Anemone; Wind Flower
Buttercup Family
Anemone occidentalis
This is a typical plant of the alpine meadow and the conspicuous white to cream flowers appear before the leaves fully expand and just as the snow melts. The delicate flowers bear numerous stamens and pistils and have attractive sepals in place of petals. The stems are stout and copiously hairy. Near the end of the short alpine summer, the blossoms are replaced by a silky, feathery head of plumy fruits, some of which hang downward suggestive of a shaggy dog. The mountain winds carry these feathery fruits over the mountain passes to new alpine sites. The generic name, *Anemone,* comes from the Greek word meaning wind. Like the related delphiniums this plant contains poisonous alkaloids (see Hardin and Arena pp. 46). This species may be seen at the delightful cirque known as Hole-in-the-wall.

Common Cowparsnip
Parsley Family
Heracleum lanatum
This hairy, perennial herb is 3 to 8 feet tall and features umbellate flower clusters 4 to 6 inches broad. It is found from the valleys to moderate elevations in the mountains on moist ground. The stems and leaves are readily eaten by a variety of large animals including grizzly and black bears. To render the stems palatable to humans, they can be peeled and boiled in two waters. However, no members of the parsley family should be eaten unless positive identification is possible. This species can be found on Boulder and Brown Pass Trails.

White Bog-orchid
Orchid Family
Habenaria dilatata
The whiteness of the small flowers makes this species easy to recognize. The lip, which has a dialated base, tapers to the tip. The spur is usually as long as the lip and projects backward from the rest of the flower. The flowers exude a striking fragrance. The angled stem is clasped by rather succulent leaves. White bog-orchid is frequently seen along stream banks or in bogs, thriving in full sun or partial shade. White bog-orchid can easily be found in wet roadside ditches along Lake McDonald or along Camas Road.

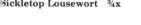

Sickletop Lousewort ¾x RJS

Western Anemone ⅓x DO

Common Cowparsnip ¼x RJS

White Bog-orchid ½x DO

Engelmann Aster

Composite Family

Aster engelmannii

Making the distinction between members of the genus, *Aster*, and the genus, *Erigeron,* is not easy. Many technical features are needed for identification. However, this species is easily recognized by such reliable criteria as disk flowers surrounded by 15 to 19 white ray flowers that may be 1 inch long. The leaves are lanceolate or elliptic and nearly smooth. The slightly hairy stem may reach a height of 3 feet. The greenish bracts, which enclose the flowers in bud, form a structure known as an involucre; and, therefore, each bract is called an involucral bract. The leaves may be boiled as greens.

Tufted Evening Primrose

Evening Primrose Family

Oenothera caespitosa

This plant is also known as moonrose, and is found on open, sunny slopes. Little or no stem is visible above the ground, but there are numerous toothed or pinnately cleft leaves. The flowers are composed of 4 sepals, 4 petals, 8 stamens, and 4 stigmas. The sweet scented blossoms are 2 to 2½ inches broad. When the flowers first open they are white but turn pink as they mature. Nectar glands are situated at the base of the hypanthium, which may be as much as 3 inches long. Only those insects, such as moths, with long mouthparts are capable of reaching the nectar. Some species in this genus have edible roots, leaves and shoots. The root is best when cooked in the spring. This species can be found along the Looking Glass Road between St. Mary and East Glacier.

Arumleaf Arrowhead

Water Plantain Family

Saggitaria cuneata

The arrowheads are plants of slow streams and ponds throughout most of North America. There is great variability in the leaves and general habit of the plants, but beneath the surface of mud or sand in which the plants are rooted, they all form rhizomes which bear starchy, tuber-like structures. The flowering stems are branched, with each branch terminating in an attractive white flower that has 3 green sepals and 3 snowy-white petals. Other common names are swamp potato, tule potato and wapatoo. The Indian women's method of gathering the tubers was unique. They entered the water hanging onto a canoe and rooted out the tubers with their toes. The dislodged tubers rose to the surface and were placed in the canoe. Lewis and Clark remarked that the tubers tasted very much like roasted potatoes. This species has been seen in Mud Lake, 4 miles south of Polebridge.

Englemann Aster   1x

Tufted Evening Primrose   ¾x

Arumleaf Arrowhead   ¾x

Fringed Grass-of-parnassus

Saxifrage Family

Parnassia fimbriata

This circumboreal species occurs at high latitudes and extends southward along mountain chains. The solitary flowers are on the ends of stems 2 to 12 inches high. The photograph emphasizes the delicately fringed bases of the petals which are so characteristic of this species. Note also that there are 5 white, fertile stamens alternating with 5 yellow, sterile stamens. The generic name refers to the mountain in Greece where the Muses of mythology lived. The plants are found in boggy places in coniferous forests and alpine meadows. Flowering occurs in July and August.

Mouse-ear Chickweed

Pink Family

Cerastium arvense

This is an extremely variable species in size and habitat sites. In moist valley areas it may be more than 12 inches tall, or in alpine habitats it may be a dwarf cushion plant. The ½ inch broad flowers have petals which are deeply notched. Close examination of the individual flowers reveal 10 minute stamens and 5 styles. Also called field chickweed, this species has swollen nodes and opposite leaves covered with velvety hairs. The generic name, *Cerastium,* comes from the Greek term meaning horn, vaguely describing the seed-capsules. This circumboreal species flowers in July and August.

White Dryas; Eight-petal Dryad

Rose Family

Dryas octopetala

Growing in limestone rocks and windy, exposed sites above tree line, this prostrate plant quickly catches one's eye because the flowers are so large (1½ inches across) and the fruits are attractive. One can readily see many adaptations to severe climatic conditions. For example, it has evergreen, leathery leaves with recurved margins to reduce water loss. It frequently grows with the tiny arctic willow. The 8 petals are responsible for the name, *octopetala,* and the name, *Dryas,* comes from the Greek word meaning wood nymph. This is a circumboreal plant, occurring in the same habitat around the world in both arctic and alpine situations. A related species, yellow mountain-aven, *D. drummondii,* forms mats in the roadside ditches near Babb, as well as along dry stream courses and river banks.

Fringed Grass-of-parnassus   1x   RJS

Mouse-ear Chickweed   1x   RJS

White Dryas   1x   RJS

Northern Bedstraw

Galium boreale

This circumboreal species is very showy and fragrant in full flower. The minute, star-like flowers lack sepals but have 4 spreading petals joined at the base. Each flower will produce 2 round, one-seeded pods which separate when they are ripe. From the rhizomes arise erect, square stems (up to 20 inches) which bear whorls of 4 narrowly lanceolate leaves. Some Indian tribes obtained a red dye from the roots; and as the common name implies, its sweet-smelling straw has been used for beds. The genus, *Galium,* belongs in the same family as true coffee. Northern bedstraw is abundant in the grasslands near the St. Mary Visitor Center and in the North Fork.

Common Yarrow

Composite Family

Achillea millefolium

Before this aromatic perennial flowers, it is sometimes mistaken for a fern because of its much divided leaves. This pinnate dissection of the leaves is responsible for the specific name, *millefolium,* meaning a thousand leaflets. The composite flowering head has both ray and disk flowers, and the corolla color is mostly white and occasionally pink. The attractive flowering heads are often used in dried plant arrangements. This plant is known throughout the northern hemisphere from sea level to the alpine tundra. With such genetic plasticity it is easy to see why several varieties have been proposed. The generic name, *Achillea,* is after Achilles who is supposed to have used yarrow to heal his wounded warriors after the siege of Troy.

White-veined Wintergreen

Wintergreen Family

Pyrola picta

The pyrolas are characterized as perennials of the cool, coniferous forest with basal leaves usually thick and leathery. The white-veined wintergreen has dark green leaves which are mottled on the upper surface with pale streaks above the main veins. The white areas of the leaves are indicative of the partial parasitic character of this and some other species of the genus. The nodding flowers have 5 sepals, 5 greenish to white petals, 10 stamens and a curving, unbranched style. A good place to find white-veined wintergreen is along the trail on the north side of St. Mary Lake.

Sitka Valerian

Valerian Family

Valeriana sitchensis

Valerians in general tend to be strongly aromatic. The roots, particularly, have a foul odor and the flowers of this species emit an oppressive odor in the autumn after the first night frost. Sitka valerian leaves are mostly on the stem, from 2 to 5 pairs in an opposite arrangement. The calyx is initially inconspicuous, but later it unrolls and enlarges to crown the fruit with numerous feathery bristles by which it becomes readily airborne. Note how the 3 stamens stand above the tubular corolla. Many wildlife species eat the leaves and stems. Many reliable accounts are given describing how members of this genus were used by Indians for food and as an antiseptic on wounds.

Northern Bedstraw ⅞x DO

Common Yarrow ¾x DO

White-veined Wintergreen ½x DO

Sitka Valerian 1x DO

Woodnymph;
One-flowered Wintergreen
Wintergreen Family
Moneses uniflora
Small, delicate perennials are to be expected in the shady, moist woods, but the slender, leafless stem bearing a single white flower of wood-nymph is indeed a surprise. The individual flowers usually face toward the ground and have a faint, pleasant odor. Several other common names, such as single delight, shy maiden and wax flower, attest to the effect of the flowers on people. The petal margins are wavy and the anthers have terminal pores for the escape of pollen. The rounded leaves form a basal rosette. This species has a wide distribution in the Rocky Mountains and extends into Alaska where it is common in the rain forests. Woodnymphs can be found around Bowman Lake and other North Fork lakes.

Mountain Lady's Slipper
Orchid Family
Cypripedium montanum
This is one of the rarest and showiest orchids of the parks, and in many parts of its range, it is threatened with extinction. The luminous, white, lower petal is strongly pouched and resembles a lady's slipper. Within the pouch 2 stamens and a pistil are fused to form a column. The rudiment of the third stamen, which forms no pollen, is the shining object in the center of the flower. The stigma is hidden from view within the pouch. The sturdy stem has parallel-veined, lanceolate leaves and may reach 18 to 20 inches in height. This species has been seen on the east side, but is more frequent on the west side, particularly in McDonald Valley and in the North Fork.

American Bistort
Buckwheat Family
Polygonum bistortoides
A frequent herb of subalpine meadows and stream banks. American bistort has a flowering stem 12 to 24 inches high. If viewed from a distance, the crowded cluster of flowers has the appearance of a tuft of wool or cotton. The individual flowers are small and bear 5 petaloid parts. The rootstocks of this species have often been used by the Indians who prized them highly for their starchy and rather pleasant taste. The rootstocks are eaten by bears and the above-ground foliage is consumed by deer and elk.

Indian-pipe
Wintergreen Family
Monotropa uniflora
The specific name, uniflora, means a single flower and the generic name, Monotropa, indicates one direction referring to the fact that the pendulous flowers are turned to one side. The above-ground stem and scale leaves are commonly white, turning black as the fruit ripens. The lack of chlorophyll in the plant indicates that no photosynthesis takes place, and nourishment must come via association with the soil fungi in the coniferous forest. Indian-pipe, while similar to pinesap, is lighter in color and has only one flower. There are three genera of the family that lack chlorophyll — Monotropa, Hypopitys and Pterospora. This species is found in McDonald Valley under cedar-hemlock forest.

Woodnymph   1x   DO

Mountain Lady's Slipper   1x   DO

American Bistort   1x   DO

Indian-pipe   1½x   DO

Bunchberry Dogwood

Dogwood Family

Cornus canadensis

This dwarf dogwood is a low growing plant with a horizontal underground stem from which arise erect branches. These short branches are 3 to 8 inches high, crowned by 5 or 6 whorled leaves with sharp points at the tips. Above the whorl of leaves is borne a cluster of cream-colored flowers surrounded by 4 white, petal-like bracts which are often mistaken for petals. After shedding bracts and flower parts, the pistils produce cardinal red fruit clusters and each berry is about ¼ inch in diameter. The leaves are eaten by the deer, and in the fall the ruffed grouse enjoy the fruit. This species grows in moist forests in the valley bottoms, especially in the North Fork Valley and McDonald Valley. Flowers appear in June.

Buckbean

Buckbean Family

Menyanthes trifoliata

This perennial grows in shallow water of bogs and lakes. The leaves are shiny and consist of 3 leaflets. However, the flowers are really different and need to be appreciated under a hand lens. The 5-petaled flowers are in an elognated, upright cluster. The individual petals are bearded with narrow hair-like scales. This circumboreal species extends south into Wyoming and Colorado, and one botanist says that buckbeans can be easily grown in garden pools. There seems to be no record of this plant being used as food. In glacier bogs it is frequently associated with *Drosera, Eriophorum,* and *Tofieldia.*

Bunchberry Dogwood ¾x   RJS

Bunchberry Dogwood ⅞x   DO

Buckbean ¾x   RJS

White Campion

Lychnis alba

This European weedy perennial (or biennial) is widely distributed in North America. It has lanceolate leaves and varies between 2 to 4 feet in height. The male and female flowers are on separate plants. Those pictured are male flowers. The white flowers open at night when night-flying moths serve as pollinating agents. Close examination of the notched petals reveals that they have appendages forming a prominent circle at a point where the corolla emerges from the fused sepals. The female flowers mature into capsules which produce a great number of small seeds. The species grows well on roadsides, waste places, and river edges.

Hood Phlox

Phlox Family

Phlox hoodii

Hood phlox is a mat-forming perennial on dry gravelly soils of the east side foothills. The leaves are awl-like, covered with soft, woolly hairs at the base and up to ½ inch long. The flowers of this genus are described as salverform, which means that the corolla has a definite tube crowned by lobes which extend at right angles. The corolla lobes are tightly twisted in bud. Blossoms occur from late April through June, and color variation ranges from white to light pink. The closely related *P. caespitosa* blooms early in the spring in dry areas such as the North Fork Valley north of Polebridge.

Bladder Campion

Pink Family

Silene cucubalus

The calyx of this perennial draws attention, not only because the 5 sepals are fused into an inflated globe, but also because of the intricate pinkish-brown veinlets. The 5 white petals are deeply two-lobed. There are 3 styles, and the flowers are perfect, meaning each flower possesses both pistil and stamens. The specific name, *cucubalis,* is derived from two Greek words meaning bad and a shot, referring to an early idea that the plant was harmful to the soil. Actually, this is a noxious weed of Eurasia that has spread rapidly through many western states. The plant's deep roots help in its survival in arid exposures of roadsides and waste places.

White Campion 1½x   DO

Hood Phlox   1x   DO

Bladder Campion   1x   DO

Broadpetal Strawberry

Fragaria virginiana

This familiar wild flower and fruit inhabits coniferous woods, meadows and stream gravels mostly at middle elevations in the mountains. Even though it lacks erect stems, it produces horizontal runners which in turn form new plants at their terminus. The flowers open in early summer and the blossoms are from ½ to 1 inch across. Each flower bears 5 green sepals, 5 rounded petals and numerous stamens. The pistils are numerous on a conical hump of tissue which becomes part of the edible fruit. The deliciously-flavored and sweet-scented fruits have been made into jams and preserves. The juicy fruits are also eaten by a number of birds and small rodents. *Fragaria vesca,* woods strawberry, also found in this area and in Europe, has yellow-green (instead of bluish-green) leaves with sunken veins and terminal teeth that are not reduced in size and recessed.

Alpine Smelowskia

Mustard Family

Smelowskia calycina

Named after an early Russian botanist, Timotheus Smelowsky, this low herb is widespread in subalpine to alpine regions of eastern Asia and western North America. The leaves of alpine smelowskia form dense tufts or mats in rocky places; the petioles are conspicuously fringed with long hairs. The flowers are arranged in short head-like racemes, becoming longer as the fruits develop. This fruit is about four times longer than it is wide. Flowering occurs in July and August. Because of the finely dissected leaf, it is also called fernleaf candytuft. This plant is common on Mt. Henry Trail.

Broadpetal Strawberry   1x   DO

Broadpetal Strawberry   1x   RJS

Alpine Smelowskia   1x   RJS

Small-flowered Woodlandstar

Lithophragma parviflora

This small, herbaceous species has most of its leaves at the base of the stem with more or less lobed leaf blades. The flowers are in racemes with pink or white petals over ¼ inch long. Note how each petal is deeply cleft into 2 to 4 narrow lobes, a feature that suggests the common name. Within the calyx and corolla there are 10 stamens. The ovary has 3 styles and forms a capsule at maturity. The generic name comes from the Greek words *lithos,* stone, and *phragma,* rock, apparently referring to the plant's habitat. Flowering occurs early in the spring in Two Medicine Valley.

Brown-eyed Susan

Composite Family

Gaillardia aristata

On sunny and well-drained slopes this perennial herb will vary from 10 to 20 inches in height. The entire plant is covered with soft hairs and is also called blanketflower. The flowering heads are borne singly on long stalks, and within the heads, the ray flowers are yellow and the disk flowers are purplish-brown. The convex receptacle of the head is covered with spine-like hairs. The species has frequently been cultivated as an ornamental garden plant. July and early August are the months in which it blooms. This species occurs on foothills and grasslands on both the west and east sides of G.N.P.

Bupleurum

Parsley Family

Bupleurum americanum

The leaves of bupleurum, also called through-wort, are simple and undivided in contrast to the many genera in this family that have finely dissected leaves. The small flowers are yellow, greenish or purplish. A hand lens will reveal that the calyx is lacking, and the fruits which develop later are slightly flattened with threadlike ribs. The fruits of this perennial consist of two parts, each containing one seed and separating from each other at maturity. The inflorescence in this family is usually called an umbel because the stalks in the flower head correspond to the ribs of an umbrella. The plant is generally found on rock outcrops at higher altitudes in Montana and Wyoming.

Small-flowered Woodlandstar   1x   DO

Brown-eyed Susan   ⅔x   GNP

Bupleurum   ¾x   RJS

Yellow Salsify; Goatsbeard

Composite Family

Tragopogon dubius

This old-world species has extensively invaded North America especially in waste places and roadside cuts. Its rapid spread is due in part
to the light, dandelion-like seeds which are carried great distances by
the wind. These coarse herbs grow from thick, biennial taproots, which
in a related species, furnish the familiar salsify or vegetable oyster.
When stems or leaves are broken, a milky juice is exuded. The flowers
of these plants open at the first light of day and close tightly about noon.
Tragopogon comes from two Greek words meaning goat and beard,
presumably referring to the conspicuous pappus at the top of the fruit.

Butter-and-eggs

Figwort Family

Linaria vulgaris

Throughout North America the butter-and-eggs plant has become a
familiar habitant of the roadsides and waste places. It closely resembles the cultivated snapdragon except that the inch-long corolla is
spurred at the base. Slender stems, 1 to 2 feet tall and bearing numerous, narrowly linear leaves, arise from perennial roots. A native of
Europe, this plant is a weed in the flax fields. In North America the
species has often escaped cultivation and formed large patches from the
creeping roots. Several other names, such as bread-and-cheese and
chopped-egg, refer to the orange and yellow corollas. Look for this plant
near Rising Sun, Many Glaciers and St. Mary.

Hairy Golden Aster

Composite Family

Chrysopsis villosa

Species of this genus resemble the genus *Aster* in a number of ways, but
differ in that the ray flowers are yellow instead of being white to purple.
One feature, visible with a hand lens, is the presence of 2 whorls of
pappus, the outer whorl being shorter than the inner whorl. Stems of
the species illustrated grow 6 to 20 inches tall. *Villosa* means hairy,
referring to the soft pubescence which covers the stem and leaves. The
covering is not sticky, however, as it is in the gumweed. This is a very
complex and confusing species consisting of several varieties differing
in pubescence and other details.

Nuttall Violet

Violet Family

Viola nuttallii

There are at least seven species of violets which bloom early in the
spring. The one pictured has a leaf slightly longer to much longer than
broad. All violets have irregular flowers consisting of 5 sepals, 5 petals
and 5 stamens. The lowest petal bears a sac-like spur at its base,
contains nectar, and in this case has brown guide lines. The whole
flower arrangement favors cross pollination. The genus, *Viola,* is considered a critical group with many difficult species, primarily because
they hybridize freely under natural conditions. Nuttall violet is found
in the drier foothills and on south facing slopes.

ellow Salsify   1x   DO

airy Golden Aster   ¾x   DO

Butter-and-eggs   1x   DO

Nuttall Violet   ⅞x   DO

Stoneseed; Columbia Puccoon

Borage Family

Lithospermum ruderale

Shoshoni women reportedly drank an infusion of stoneseed roots every day to act as a contraceptive. Experiments using alcoholic extracts of the plant on mice eliminated the estrous cycle, thus verifying in part the Indian use. This perennial has a clump of hairy stems and lanceolate leaves, 1 to 4 inches long. The flowers are in small clusters in the upper axils of the leaves. The pale yellow corolla is often greenish tinted. The plant grows in dry places up to mid-elevations in the mountains. The generic name, *Lithospermum,* comes from two Greek words, stone and seed, a reference to the very hard stony seeds. This species is found in grasslands and dry woodlands on the east side. It is also common in dry meadows and prairies and the North Fork.

Prairie Coneflower

Composite Family

Ratibida columnifera

The common name, coneflower, refers to the column or cone of tiny disc flowers in the center of the composite flower head. The yellow ray flowers are up to 1½ inches long, often hanging down. These ray flowers immediately set it apart from the more widespread western coneflower of the genus, *Rudbeckia.* Prairie Indians gathered the leaves and flower heads for a tea-like beverage and as a yellow-orange dye. This perennial species has spread east and west of the Central States where it is a common prairie plant.

Mullein

Figwort Family

Verbascum thapsus

This biennial plant is silvery green in color and is covered with soft hairs making it velvet-like to the touch. The first year the plant produces a basal rosette of thick leaves, and the second year it forms a flowering stalk up to 6 feet tall. The flowers are nearly regular which is unusual for this family since most members of the family have bilaterally symmetrical blossoms. After flowering, the dead stems may persist for a year or more, changing to a dark brown color. Mullein is an alien species of Eurasia which inhabits disturbed sites along roads.

Glacier Lily

Lily Family

Erythronium grandiflorum

Common names of plants frequently cause confusion among flower lovers because they vary so much in different geographical areas. For example, this plant is also known as dogtooth violet, adder's tongue, fawn lily and trout lily. In both parks the plants are abundant on east and west slopes. The yellow, nodding flowers are on a stem 6 to 12 inches high. This stem arises from a bulb several inches below the soil surface. In this area almost all of the flowers have yellow anthers but a few have red anthers. At maturity the seed pods are erect. In some areas, notably in the North Fork between Quartz and Camas Creeks, the flowers are pale yellow to white. The flowers open early in the season while the snow is still melting and attract much attention at Logan Pass. Grizzly bears dig up the edible bulbs.

oneseed 1x   DO   **Prairie Coneflower ¾x**   RJS

ullein 1x   DO   **Glacier Lily ¾x**   DO

Evening Primrose

Oenothera hookeri

This is a difficult genus in which species identification can be frustrating. All species have an inferior ovary and a long hypanthium (fused bases of sepals, petals and stamens) which serves to elevate the showy petals, stamens and stigma above the lanceolate leaves. The anthers are balanced on the filaments at their mid-point and thus are able to swing to and fro in the wind. The tall style is topped by a stigma that is divided into 4 finger-like lobes which spread star-like. Nectar glands are positioned at the base of the hypanthium and this means that only those insects with long mouthparts can reach the sweet liquid reward.

Heartleaf Arnica

Arnica cordifolia

This aromatic perennial inhabits coniferous forests throughout the Rocky Mountain region and has received its common name from the fact that basal and lower stem leaves are markedly heart-shaped at the base. Blossoming begins in mid-June and lasts until mid-July. A few individuals start to bloom again in early September. The dried flowerheads of *Arnica montana,* a European species, have been used since the sixteenth century as a treatment for bruises and sprains. Ten other species of Arnica occur in both parks. Heartleaf arnica is very abundant in lodgepole pine forests.

Yellow Columbine

Aquilegia flavescens

The 5 long tubes or "spurs" of the columbine flower are really petals. There are 5 pistils and many stamens. The scientific name seems to be derived from the Latin word, *aquila,* meaning eagle. Apparently the spurred petals suggest an eagle's talons. The leaves are divided into many small segments. These plants inhabit streamsides in moist mountain meadows, alpine slopes and some roadside cuts. The old herbals of Europe mention many medicinal uses of columbine leaves, and the Indians used the boiled roots as a cure for diarrhea.

Dwarf Mountain Butterweed; Groundsel

Senecio fremontii

As a genus, *Senecio,* is one of the largest genera of the flowering plants, having at least 1,000 species described. At least 13 species occur in both parks. These species have yellow to yellow-orange flowers in heads bearing both ray and disk flowers. Senecios might be confused with arnicas, but the latter species have lower leaves that are opposite while groundsels have alternate leaves. The generic name, *Senecio,* is derived from the Latin, *senix,* meaning old man, probably referring to the white pappus or hoary pubescence of some species. The species illustrated occupies rocky places at high elevations.

vening Primrose ½x   DO

Heartleaf Arnica ¾x   RJS

ellow Columbine ½x   RJS

Dwarf Mountain Butterweed ¾x   DO

Balsamroot

Composite Family

Balsamorhiza sagittata

The June visitors frequently confuse this common plant with the sunflower, but careful examination reveals many striking differences. Numerous basal leaves are arrowhead-shaped and covered with tiny, silvery hairs. When the balsamroot is abundant along the highway, many folks comment about its pungent odor. The stems are 1 to 2 feet tall, bearing solitary heads of yellow flowers at their termini. It is located in open, sunny areas from low to mid-elevations. The plants, especially the tender shoots, are eaten by mountain sheep, deer and elk.

Common Bladderwort

Bladderwort Family

Utricularia vulgaris

This circumboreal species has submerged floating stems and leaves. The leaves are divided into thin linear segments which bear small bladders of unique construction. The hollow bladders are fitted with a valve that is normally open. When microscopic aquatic animals swim into the bladders, they trip certain guard-hairs so the valves close. The walls of the bladder then secrete digestive juices and the nitrogenous compounds in the animal's bodies are utilized by the plants. From the submerged stem rises an erect flowering stem up to 4 inches tall. Note the similarity of the yellow flowers to those of butter-and-eggs. The generic name comes from the latin, *utriculus,* meaning a small bag and referring to the hollow bladders which trap aquatic animals. Look for the plant in Mud Lake, four miles south of Polebridge.

Mountain Goldenpea

Pea Family

Thermopsis montana

Because of a superficial resemblance, this plant is frequently called false lupine, but several distinctive features set it apart. The leaves are trifoliately compound with leaflets up to 4 inches long. The 10 stamens are always separate and distinct. As the petals fall off, the ovary elongates, and at maturity the flat fruits may be erect or horizontal. Goldenpea is unpalatable to game and grazing livestock so it may replace more desirable forage plants. There are reports that this legume contains a number of toxic alkaloids especially in the seeds. It inhabits wet meadows, well-drained soils and dry forest sites. Flowers are seen in May along Highway 2 near East Glacier.

Balsamroot ¼x RJS

Common Bladderwort ¾x RJS

Mountain Goldenpea ¾x RJS

Yellow Pondlily; Spatterdock

Waterlily Family

Nuphar polysepalum

This perennial herb grows from submerged rhizomes and bears long-petioled leaves usually floating on the surface. The showy, regulary flowers are from 2 to 3 inches in diameter, having 7 to 12 sepals and many stamen-like petals. The sagittately-lobed leaf blades are 5 to 12 inches long and 5 to 9 inches broad. The capsule fruit bear many seeds which are eaten by ducks. The Indians of Montana parched the seeds or ground them into flour. The rhizomes, too, were eaten but had to be collected from the muddy bottoms of ponds in a similar manner to the collecting of arrowhead rhizomes by using the toes.

Mountain Buttercup

Buttercup Family

Ranunculus eschscholtzii

This low herb with clustered stems and showy yellow cups should evoke wonder and amazement when contrasted with the savage environmental conditions of its inhospitable perch, high on alpine slopes. The 5 yellow sepals give way to broad, overlapping petals that are strikingly waxy. All flowers have numerous stamens and pistils. There are several varieties of this species in western North America that are separated on the variation of the basal leaves. In a superficial way, yellow buttercups resemble cinquefoils, but can be easily separated by looking for the tiny sac or scale-covered gland at the base of the petals of buttercups. At least 12 species of *Ranunculus* occur in the two parks. This species appears early in the spring on Piegan Pass Trail.

Missouri Goldenrod

Composite Family

Solidago missouriensis

It is difficult to separate the many species of goldenrods found in North America because the genus has a lack of consistent distinguishing characteristics. The species are all erect perennials, bearing alternate leaves and small composite heads containing both disk and ray flowers. The many, small flowering heads are arranged on only one side of the spreading branches. The flowering period is in August and September, and this species grows in a variety of dry, open sites. A persistent belief that goldenrods are hay-fever plants has been discredited by studies that show the pollen is relatively heavy, and therefore dispersed poorly by the wind.

Yellow Pondlily ½x RJS

•

Mountain Buttercup 1x DO

Missouri Goldenrod ¾x RJS

Large-leaved Avens
Geum macrophyllum

Large-leaved avens has flowers resembling those of the cinquefoils, having 5 bracts, 5 reflexed sepals, 5 petals, and numerous stamens and pistils. It is the leaves and styles that set this species apart. The basal leaves are pinnately compound and equipped with terminal segments many times larger than the lateral lobes. The lengthened style is kinked at a joint, so that when the uper hairy part falls off, the lower part ends in a hook. As the numerous achenes mature, they form a spherical bur with hooked prickles. Such an arrangement is very effective for dispersal. This species inhabits streambanks, moist woods, and even disturbed sites.

Round-leaved Violet
Viola orbiculata

The flower structure of violets is complex and must be interpreted in terms of adaptation to pollination. The lower petal is extended backward into a hollow spur. The 2 lower stamens bear the nectar-secreting glands which are enclosed within the spur. The guide lines on the petals and the arrangement of all flower parts favor cross-fertilization; yet, in many violets self-fertilizing flowers that never open are produced later in the season. The species illustrated has round, glabrous leaves which persist through the winter. Occurring in moist forests up to moderately high elevations, this is the most widespread violet in the northern Rockies. Stream violet, *V. glabella,* is often found with round-leaved violet on more moist sites.

American Globeflower
Trollius laxus

This smooth, perennial herb bears its large, conspicuous flowers singly at the ends of its several stems. There are no petals, but the 5 to 8 cream-colored sepals are often ½ inch long. The basal leaves have blades which are divided into 5 lobes or segments. At the base of the petioles are broad sheathing stipules. The fruits in this species are follicles with several seeds. These plants inhabit swampy ground to alpine meadows, generally blossoming near melting snow. Flowers appear from May through August.

Large-leaved Avens   1x

Round-leaved Violet   ¾x

American Globeflower   1x

Snow Cinquefoil

Potentilla nivea

This dwarf perennial species may be found on rocky slopes and high altitude moraines. The most conspicuous alpine adaptation displayed by the plant is the long, soft hairs covering the stems and leaves. These hairs protect the plant's stomata, the pores through which the gasses are exchanged. The hairs also reduce the intensity and directness of strong alpine light. *Potentilla* is a large and taxonomically difficult genus of at least 200 species. Recognition of the genus, however, is easy. Below the 5 sepals are 5 bracts which seem like an extra calyx. Because of the 5 yellow petals and many pistils and stamens, the cinquefoils might be mistaken for buttercups or even roses, but the extra calyx (the subtending bracts) make the difference.

Lance-leaved Stonecrop

Sedum lanceolatum

Because of the succulent nature of their leaves and stems, the recognition of the genus *Sedum* is easy, but the separation of the species is confusing, calling for careful attention to details. Lance-leaved stonecrop has numerous basal leaves. The leaves on the stem vary greatly in shape, and they are not ridged underneath. Each flower, resembling a bright yellow star, has 5 petals, 8-10 stamens and 5 pistils which form 5 follicles when mature. Look for this species on rocks and gravelly soil, extending from the forest upward into the alpine. Flowers occur from late June through August, depending on elevation. Roseroot, *S. rosea,* is another species which is attractive in the alpine area.

Large Yellow Monkeyflower

Mimulus tilingii

Fragile beauty characterizes this perennial herb of wet meadows and stream banks. The bright yellow corolla with its delicate hairs and orange spots helps to attract insect pollinators. Examination of the stigma with a hand lens reveals 2 roundish lobes which are spread apart. When one of these lobes makes contact with a pollen-laden insect, the 2 stigma lobes immediately fold together like the leaves of a book. The pollen will thus be held firmly, and when the insect backs out of the corolla, no self-pollination will occur. This species often grows with *M. lewisii* at higher elevations. Four other species of this genus are also present in the parks.

Snow Cinquefoil   1x   DO

Lance-leaved Stonecrop   ¾x   DO

Yellow Monkeyflower   ⅛x   DO

Bracted Lousewort; Indian Warrior
Figwort Family

Pedicularis bracteosa

This species produces a tall stem up to 40 inches high and has pinnately divided fern-like leaves. The flowers are in a terminal spike. The individual flowers are ½ to ¾ inch long and are curved downward at the tip. The corolla varies from yellow to reddish. Indian warrior grows in open woods and moist alpine meadows. Elk are reported to eat the flowers and stems at the time of flowering in late June and July. Pollination in this genus is complex, usually requiring a specific bee pollinator.

Common Tansy
Composite Family

Tanacetum vulgare

Common tansy is an old world perennial which was cultivated as a medicinal plant in North America and escaped. The stems vary from 2 to 4 feet tall and are topped by flat clusters of rayless, yellow flower heads. The finely dissected leaves are strongly pungent. The Europeans officially used tansy to induce menstruation, and the Indians utilized a tea made from the plant to induce abortion (sometimes with disastrous results). Look for this widely naturalized species in disturbed sites during August and September, particularly near the old St. Mary Ranger Station and in front of the Two Medicine campstore.

Western St. Johnswort
St. Johnswort Family

Hypericum formosum

During the middle ages, the European herbalists developed many superstitions and medicinal properties in connection with the common St. Johnswort of Europe which later migrated to America. There are several American species which are usually found at middle and high altitudes. The species at the right has an elongated, open inflorescence, and the unopened flower buds are conspicuously red in contrast to the yellow mature flowers. Under a hand lens the leaves show small, black dots on the margins. This species is abundant in the Logan Pass area.

Yellowbell; Yellow Fritillary
Lily Family

Fritillaria pudica

Depending on elevation, the flowering stem appears in late May or June in the sagebrush or woodland areas. The yellow, nodding flowers become more orange with aging. The perianth parts are about ¾ inch long, and when they fall off, the stem straightens out, placing the 3-sectioned fruit in an erect position. The underground bulbs are 2 to 6 inches beneath the surface and reproduce asexually by forming tiny offsets the size of rice grains. While the bulbs and offsets are edible, either raw or cooked, such use should be discouraged because bulbous plants can be eliminated by heavy usage. Flowers appear in April at low elevations on both sides of the parks.

...racted Lousewort   ¾x   RJS

Common Tansy   1x   RJS

...estern St. Johnswort   1¼x   DO

Yellowbell   1x   DO

Wood Lily

Lilium philadelphicum

Of about 20 species growing in North America, the wood lily and the Columbia lily, *L. columbianum,* are the only true lilies found in the Rocky Mountains. The flowers are erect at the top of the stem, either one or several in a group. The perianth members are orange-red to brick-red and are narrowly tapered at the base, thus not concealing the ovary. The inner portion of the petals are beautifully spotted with a maroon-wine color. This species is not recorded in G.N.P., but is seen in W.N.P., especially near the western terminus of Chief Mountain Road. This spectacular species which may reach 4 feet, could disappear if thoughtless admirers pluck the stems. It is found in more or less alkaline meadows to montane forests, especially in aspen groves.

Orange Agoseris

Composite Family

Agoseris aurantiaca

Sometimes called false dandelion, this plant is found in timberline areas and grassy situations in coniferous forests. The solitary composite head is located on a leafless, erect stem up to 20 inches high. The stem and the basal leaves exude a milky juice when broken. All the flowers in the head are the ray type. The fruits which follow have soft, white hairs that aid in dispersal. The specific name, *aurantiaca,* is derived from the Latin meaning orange. Agoseris species, like true dandelions, have been used for food, such as greens and beverages.

Prairiesmoke

Rose Family

Geum triflorum

The nodding flowers and the heads of feathery styles have been responsible for many common names, such as old-man's whiskers, long-plumed avens and china bells. The stems are from 7 to 18 inches high and have mostly basal and fern-like leaves. The whole plant is softly hairy, and this feature makes it challenging as a photographic subject. The fruits are dispersed by the winds catching the long feathery styles. The Blackfeet Indians are reported to have used the root of this plant as an eye wash. Look for the flowers in May and June in open meadows, hillsides and ridges.

Lyall's Rockcress

Mustard Family

Arabis lyallii

Members of the mustard family are distinctive because of their cross-shaped flowers formed by 4 petals and the adroecium combination of 2 short and 4 long stamens. Also called crucifers, these plants have flowers in racemes and usually 2-chambered fruits. The rockcress pictured represents a difficult genus, the species of which cannot be identified without fruits and basal leaves. The basal leaves in this species lack teeth and are narrow. The stem leaves are well separated and generally lack basal lobes. The fruits are nearly erect and sharply pointed. Look for this crucifer on ridges and rocky meadows at high altitudes.

Wood Lily ¼x   DO

Orange Agoseris 1x   DO

Prairiesmoke 1x   DO

Lyall's Rockcress 1¼x   DO

Pink Dogbane

Dogbane Family

Apocynum androsaemifolium

This is a freely branching semi-shrub growing to a height of 24 inches. When broken, the stems and leaves exude an acrid milky juice. The opposite leaves are egg-shaped with a short pointed tip. These leaves often droop during the heat of the afternoon. The small, bell-shaped flowers are pink, attractively lined with darker pink guide lines. Five stamens are arranged around a pistil with 5 nectaries at its base. The fruiting capsules are pendulous and up to 3 inches long. This plant is common on dry, disturbed sites, but it can also grow in cool, moist forests. Look for it on roadside cuts from Polebridge to Kintla Lake.

Twinflower

Honeysuckle Family

Linnaea borealis

Linnaeus, the father of modern plant toxonomy, had a favorite flower, the twinflower, and in 1737 this plant was named to honor him. This creeping evergreen herb is found in open to dense, moist coniferous woods and has a circumboreal distribution. From the trailing branches rise flower stalks which bear 2 pendant pink flowers. The corolla of the slender bell-shaped blossoms is almost equally 5-lobed, but there are only 4 stamens. Its tiny dry fruits are sticky because of hooked bristles which become readily attached to animals and birds.

Field Mint

Mint Family

Mentha arvensis

The mint family can be easily recognized by three characteristics — irregular flowers, square stems and opposite leaves. However, because the flowers of most species are small, it is difficult to separate the genera without checking minute details of stamens and other technical features. The flowers of field mint are in the axils of foliage leaves. The corolla is mostly 4-lobed; the upper lobe is notched and usually broader than the others. The plants of this genus secrete aromatic, volatile oils used as medicines and flavoring agents — e.g., menthol, peppermint and spearmint. Wet woods and streambanks are typical habitats for this species, especially along North Fork streams. Flowers are evident from July through September.

Showy Milkweed

Milkweed Family

Asclepias speciosa

From their milky juice found in stems and leaves to their ornate and complex flowers, the milkweeds are strange plants well separated from other families. This species of milkweed is the most abundant of the Rocky Mountain region, occupying roadsides and moist streambanks. The flowers are unique and must be examined critically with a hand lens to appreciate the insect-flower relationship that has evolved in the genus. Each flower has 5 sepals, 5 petals, 5 stamens and 2 separate ovaries except for fusion at the apex. Each fruit (follicle) splits down one side at maturity, liberating relatively large seeds with silk-like hairs at one end. All milkweeds are highly specialized for insect pollination. The pollen grains are sticky and hang together in masses called pollinia.

114

Pink Dogbane 1x   DO

Twinflower ¾x   DO

Field Mint ⅔x   DO

Showy Milkweed ½x   DO

Narrow-leaf Collomia

Phlox Family

Collomia linearis

The generic name, *Collomia,* means glue and refers to the mucilagin-
ous quality of the moistened seeds. Like other members of the phlox
family, the flowers are gamopetalous — i.e., with petals joined in a
well-developed corolla tube, usually with 5 lobes. Disturb a coniferous
forest or prairie site with a road, and one of the first annual species to
invade will be the narrow-leaf collomia. The stem varies from 4 to 15
inches high, according to moisture. The pink, tubular flowers may
reach ½ inch long and form dense clusters in axils of leafy bracts. The
calyx tube is papery in texture and enlarges as the fruit matures. This
species is found on roadsides in North Fork Valley.

Moss Campion; Carpet Pink

Pink Family

Silene acaulis

The small branches of this perennial plant form a tightly interwoven
cushion connecting to a deep penetrating taproot. In the alpine tundra
such a growth habit raises the temperature inside the cushion and
helps to create a micro-climate which is more suitable for survival.
Sometimes in the older cushions, seeds of other plants germinate and
gradually become established. At first glance the plant may seem to
resemble a dwarf *Phlox* but the petals of the moss campion are distinct
and separate, whereas they are united in the *Phlox*. Also known as the
moss pink, this plant may be 10 years old before it begins to flower.
Many plants are found along the trail to Swiftcurrent Lookout. This
species is frequent in many alpine areas such as Two Medicine Pass and
Dawson Pass.

Creeping Thistle; Canada Thistle

Composite Family

Cirsium arvense

This Eurasian invader is now a cosmopolitan weed mainly because it
not only produces parachute-like seeds, but it also forms creeping
rhizomes that produce dense continuous populations. The plants are 2
to 5 feet high and bear numerous small heads. The pinkish-purple
flowers add a decorative touch to some roadside cuts. The creeping
thistle is unique among thistles of our area in that most of the plants
are dioecious — i.e., staminate and pistillate flowers are found on
different individuals. The flowers of the composite heads are filled with
nectar and attract a variety of pollinating agents. Young leaves, tender
roots or flower heads may be used for food in times of emergency. The
two parks have about five species, some of which are difficult to identify. Horses are very fond of thistles, particularly elk thistle.

Narrow-leaf Collomia   1x   RJS

Moss Campion   1¼x   MM

Creeping Thistle   1x   RJS

Fireweed
Evening Primrose Family
Epilobium angustifolium
Fireweed rapidly invades burned over and logged areas with a beautiful cover of deep pink flowers. The reddish stems, bearing many alternate, lance-like leaves, may reach a height of 6 feet. The slightly irregular flowers are constructed on a plan of four. In the fall, the slender inflorescences take on a fluffy, white appearance because the tips of the seeds are covered with long, white hairs. The forests in this area are showered annually with the airborne seeds of this plant. Successful invasion, however, depends on the reduced plant competition of disturbed sites. Boiling young shoots like asparagus is one way to use fireweed for food. This plant can be seen with hollyhock on the 1967 burn on Going-to-the-Sun Road.

Wild Bergamont; Horsemint; Bee Balm
Mint Family
Monarda fistulosa
Wild bergamont is easily recognized by several features; opposite leaves, square stems, bilabiate corolla and a pleasant mint odor. The long style and 2 stamens are exserted from the upper lip of the corolla. It is found in moist, open places up to mid-elevations in the mountains, and its height varies from 12 to 24 inches. A number of authors comment about this species being used as a plant remedy by the Indians, especially to relieve bronchial complaints and skin disorders. The plant is common along roads on the east side foothills.

Alpine Fireweed; Willowherb
Evening Primrose Family
Epilobium latifolium
This circumboreal species pioneers on gravelly or sandy floodplains or on talus in the mountains. Like other evening primroses, the individual flowers of this species have evolved on a plan of four — 4 sepals, 4 magenta petals, 8 stamens and 4 stigmatic lobes. The 3 to 12 flowers are in short racemes with leafy bracts. Flowering begins in late July and continues into early September. The fruits are slender, 4-chambered capsules with numerous seeds, each bearing a tuft of soft, white hairs at the tip. The fleshy, young leaves taste like spinach when cooked. In the northern Rockies this plant is usually found near timberline.

Elephanthead
Figwort Family
Pedicularis groenlandica
Close examination of a single flower will reveal why this plant has such a descriptive common name. The upper lip of the corolla has a long upcurving beak. Two petals of the lower lip are shaped like ears. Together the parts of this irregular flower have an amazing resemblance to an elephant's head. The leaves are all pinnately divided. Look for the purple spikes in wet meadows and along streams. It is quite common in lowland moist areas and even appears above timberline. It blooms during July and August.

Fireweed ½x   DO

Wild Bergamont ¾x   DO

Alpine Fireweed 1x   DO   Elephanthead 1x   DO

Rocky Mountain Douglasia

Douglasia montana

Most visitors probably won't see this early bloomer (May to June), but to see this cushion-forming species ablaze with pink flowers is worth the wait and effort needed to find it. Like other true primroses, this *Douglasia* has an angular calyx with 5 teeth. The corolla is in the form of a tube with 5 flaring lobes. The stamens are attached to the inside of the corolla tube and never project above the tube. Cushion plants are well adapted to severe environments, and the cushion is often invaded by other species because the compacted mass of leaves and branches form a suitable site for seed germination. Look for this species in the foothills along the road from St. Mary to East Glacier. It also gets as high as Firebrand Pass.

Water Smartweed; Ladysthumb

Buckwheat Family

Polygonum amphibium

This plant is a perennial with floating or submerged stems. The leaves are oblong-elliptic, smooth, and 2 to 4 inches long. In the axils of the leaves adventitious roots are formed. The minute flowers have 4 to 6 sepals and from 4 to 9 stamens arranged around 2 styles. The clusters of flowers have reminded some visitors of a painted fingernail. This species is frequent in the two parks in shallow ponds and muddy lake edges. As the scientific name implies, it is at home on land or in the water; however, this form is usually aquatic. Water smartweed occurs on every continent except Australia.

Sticky Geranium

Geranium Family

Geranium viscosissimum

This beautiful herbaceous species is found in sagebrush, grasslands and open woods. It has strong branching stems from 10-30 inches tall and deeply-lobed leaves. The rose-purple flowers (1-1½ inches across) are constructed on a plan of five — i.e., all parts are five in number, or multiples of five. The capsule-like fruit, typical of the family, is beaked due to the elongation of the style. As the capsule ripens, its longitudinal sections split open with such recoiling force that the seeds are catapulted outward from the parent plant for several feet. Stems, leaves and some flower parts are covered with sticky, glandular hairs. White geranium, *G. richardsonii*, may be found in aspen groves on both sides of the parks.

Rocky Mountain Douglasia ¾x   DO

Water Smartweed ¾x   RJS

Sticky Geranium 1¼x   RJS

Globemallow; Mountain Hollyhock
Mallow Family
Iliamna rivularis

Along streams and roadsides the large pink flowers add their distinctive color during July and August. The stems are stout, branched and reach a height of 4 or 5 feet. The maplelike leaves are 2 to 8 inches across, generally with 5 lobes. The individual flowers are up to 2 inches broad and resemble the cultivated hollyhocks. Irritating hairs cover the fruits which break open like segments of oranges. In some areas of the Rocky Mountains this is one of the first herbaceous species to appear after a forest fire. Look for this plant along the Going-to-the-Sun Highway between St. Mary and Rising Sun, also in the area of the 1967 fire below the tunnel on the west side of Logan Pass.

Pygmy Bitterroot; Breadroot
Purslane Family
Lewisia pygmaea

The genus, *Lewisia,* was named in honor of Capt. Lewis of the Lewis and Clark Expedition, and this species is similar to the Montana state flower, the bitterroot, except that it is much smaller (less than 3 inches high) and bears live succulent leaves while in bloom. The petal number varies from 5 to 9, and the color ranges from white to deep pink and lavender. This much overlooked species blooms only in July and August and inhabits moist to dry places in the mountains and even survives above timberline. Often the plant can be found on rock ledges in the Logan Pass area and in exposed places high up in the Apgar Mountains.

Western Springbeauty
Purslane Family
Claytonia lanceolata

Springbeauties are widely recognized across North America as flowers that follow retreating snowbanks. Usually several stems grow from a tuberous underground corm. Each of these stems has 2 succulent leaves. Flower color varies from white to pink, and in the whiter forms, pinkish veins add emphasis to the notched petals. There are 2 sepals persisting long after petal fall. The tuberous corms (½ to ¾ inches in diameter) were dug by the Indians and eaten as we would eat potatoes. These plants are frequent in meadows of subalpine and alpine areas. Alpine springbeauty, *C. megarhiza,* with pink flowers and numerous leaves can be found above timberline on talus slopes such as those near Siyeh Pass. Except for *Trillium* this is the earliest blooming flower.

Globemallow   1x   MM

Pygmy Bitterroot   1¼x   DO

Western Springbeauty   1x   RJS

Fairy Slipper; Calypso Orchid

Orchid Family

Calypso bulbosa var. *americana*

The Waterton-Glacier area has at least 18 species of orchids, but this is one of the most beautiful and striking. It grows in deep shaded areas of the coniferous forest and blooms early in the season. Usually it has only one small, green, basal leaf which, along with the stem, arises from a bulbous corm, embedded frequently in decaying wood or organic matter. The flower resembles a small lady's slipper with its cup-like lip. Luer (see references) says the flowers are odorless and have no nectar.

Clarkia; Pink Fairies

Evening Primrose Family

Clarkia pulchella

Clarkia is named for Capt. William Clark of the Lewis and Clark Expedition; the species name, *pulchella,* means beautiful. A close examination of the flower reveals a startling design constructed on a plan of four. The 4 petals are strongly 3-lobed and have a pair of teeth at the base. The 4 lobes of the stigma are generally white and almost petal-like. This annual species is found in moderately dry sites from western Montana to British Columbia and southeastern Oregon. A number of species of this genus are grown in gardens, some under the name godetia.

Prince's Pine; Pipsissewa

Wintergreen Family

Chimaphila umbellata

This plant is a trailing and somewhat woody perennial with wax-glossed evergreen leaves. The flowers, borne in small, umbellate clusters, are pink and contain 10 distinctive stamens radiating around the fat, green ovary. The fruits are roundish capsules holding numerous small seeds. If a hand lens is used to look at the stamens, the purple anthers reveal terminal pores through which pollen is shed much as salt grains come out of a salt shaker. The name, *pipsissewa,* is evidently of Indian origin, and the plant was used for a wide variety of ailments, such as rheumatism and fevers.

Thin-leaved Owl-clover

Figwort Family

Orthocarpus tenuifolius

Owl-clovers resemble the Indian paintbrushes, *Castilleja,* in a number of features. They are small, annual plants up to 15 inches tall. The yellow flowers are borne in the axils of bracts which, in this species, are rose-pink and petal-like. The overlapping, linear leaves blend into the bracts in the flower spike. Another species, *O. luteus,* has green bracts and is the most common species in the Rocky Mountains. The species pictured grows in open woods and on prairie sites, blooming from May through August, especially in the grasslands near St. Mary.

airy Slipper ¾x   DO

Clarkia 1¼   DO

'rince's Pine 1¼x   DO   **Thin-leaved Owl-clover 1x**   DO

Sticky Shooting Star
Primrose Family
Dodecatheon cusickii
The sticky shooting star is similar to the cultivated cyclamen having petals which are reflexed backward. The generic name, *Dodecatheon,* comes from two Greek words, *dodeka,* meaning twelve and *theos,* meaning God, or literally, plants protected by the gods. Careful examination of this striking flower with a hand lens will reveal that the stamens are opposite the corolla lobes, a feature quite different from most families. The flowering stalk varies between 7 and 14 inches high. This species blooms early in the spring at low elevations and much later at higher elevations.

Northern Sweetvetch
Pea Family
Hedysarum boreale
Since the flowers of this species closely resemble those of milkvetches and locoweeds, it is prudent to look for the fruit to verify identification. Sweetvetch pods are flattened and are remarkably constricted between the seeds so that each section appears almost round. The other mentioned plants have typical fruits shaped like garden peas. Inhabiting gravelly or sandy soil in stream channels or terraces in both parks, this plant is found from mid to high elevations, usually in grassland vegetation. The keel of the flower is nearly straight and longer than the wings.

Lewis Monkeyflower
Figwort Family
Mimulus lewisii
Hiking the high canyon trails from 7,000 feet to 9,000 feet, one is very likely to see the Lewis monkeyflower growing very close to some small stream. It was named after Lewis of the Lewis and Clark Expedition. Captain Lewis found this plant near Glacier Park in 1805. The 5 petals of the flower are united into a tube with spreading corolla lobes. Such structure is well adapted to pollination by bees. When a bee crawls into the wide opening of the corolla for nectar, its back becomes dusted with pollen which it carries to the next flower. As the bee crawls into the tube of the second flower, its back brushes pollen onto the stigma.

Pink Pyrola; Shinleaf
Wintergreen Family
Pyrola asarifolia
The nodding flowers are light pink to purplish and are arranged in slender racemes on stems 8 to 15 inches high. There are 5 petals and 10 stamens, the anthers of which release their pollen through terminal pores. The kidney-shaped leaves are basal and are relatively thick and shiny. Look for this evergreen perennial in wet soil around streams and in the shade of coniferous forests. The fruit is a dry capsule. Several other pyrolas are present in the northern Rockies.

ticky Shooting Star 1x   DO

Northern Sweetvetch 1x   DO

ewis Monkeyflower 1x   DO

Pink Pyrola 1x   DO

Common Indian Paintbrush

Figwort Family

Castilleja miniata

The actual flowers of the plant are narrow, tubular and greenish-yellow. The vivid scarlet of the leafy bracts provide the color of the most common species, and yet there are several species in the parks whose bracts are white, yellow, orange, or pink. The plants bloom from mid-June to early September. This is the most common species and it grows in moist and shady places in the mountains. Wyoming has chosen one species of *Castilleja* as its state flower, *C. linariaefolia*.

Rhexia-leaved Paintbrush

Figwort Family

Castilleja rhexifolia

Identification of the park's eight species of *Castilleja* can be quite frustrating, and it really takes a botanical specialist working with technical details to separate them. Minute details about the bracts, calyx and corolla must be considered. In all *Castilleja* species the corolla has a narrow, folded upper lip, called the galea, and a lower lip with 3 lobes or teeth. *Castilleja rhexifolia* reaches up to 12 inches and bears leaves which are narrowly lanceolate. It inhabits high mountain meadows and blooms during July and August. At least some of the species are reported to be partial parasites on the roots of a number of other plants. The paintbrush plants on Boulder Pass and other alpine areas are particularly attractive.

Marsh Cinquefoil

Rose Family

Potentilla palustris

The common name, cinquefoil, means five leaves and is used for all species regardless of the number of leaf segments. The scientific name, *Potentilla,* means the little potent one because of the supposedly medicinal value of one species. *P. palustris* is the only species with red petals. The 20-40 inch stems may be prostrate or floating in water. *Palustris* means marshy or boggy and this species is found at the edge of lakes and wet meadows. The roots are edible, either boiled or roasted, and taste like parsnips or sweet potatoes.

Common Indian Paintbrush   1x   RJS

Rhexia-leaved Paintbrush   1x   RJS

Marsh Cinquefoil   1x   RJS

Waterleaf

Hydrophyllum capitatum

The first visitors of each travel season will find this handsome plant along with violets and springbeauties, especially in wooded areas. The light violet flowers (about ⅜ inch long) are in a dense, ball-like cluster which has a fringed appearance because the anthers and bilobed stigmas are held conspicuously above the corolla. The species name, *capitatum,* means a head and refers to the flower cluster. *Hydrophyllum* means water-leaf, but the meaning in this case is obscure. The species is variable and widely distributed from the Canadian Rockies southward into Utah and Colorado. This plant blooms in May in the North Fork area, and the flowering head is sometimes hidden by the leaves that are higher on the stem.

Wild Blue Flax; Lewis Flax

Linum perenne var. *lewisii*

Wild blue flax inhabits dry soils of prairie flats or subalpine ridges. The numerous flowers are located on very slender stems which bend and bow to every passing breeze. The 5 blue petals are extremely fragile and will fall off at the slightest handling. Unthinking flower pickers will be sadly disappointed five minutes after plucking a handful of these delicate plants. The blossoms open early in the morning and usually close late in the afternoon. The brown seed capsules, about ¼ inch across, contain numerous seeds that are rich in oil. *L. usitatissimum* was cultivated in very ancient times in Egypt and Eurasia. Indians of the Pacific Northwest used the plant to manufacture their thread and fishing tackle. This species is common on the North Fork savannahs.

Alpine Forget-me-not

Eritrichium nanum

Many cushion plants occur in the alpine tundra, but brilliant blue flowers and delicate fragrance make this cushion plant unforgettable. One open flower is considerably smaller than a thumbtack, and when a bumblebee visits the flower, its body covers the entire perianth. Note the yellow center of the corolla which leads to the hidden stamens. The fruit consists of 4 nutlets. Cushion plants in general reach only a few inches above the surface, and as a result, avoid the harsh environmental conditions of high elevations. The generic name, *Eritrichium,* means woolly hair in reference to woolly pubescence of the leaves. This is another mountain species that has a circumboreal distribution, and can be found on East Flattop Mountain.

Waterleaf 1x   RJS

Wild Blue Flax 1x   RJS

Alpine Forget-me-not 1x   RJS

Alpine Speedwell

Figwort Family

Veronica wormskjoldii

Members of the genus *Veronica* have lower, opposite leaves and distinctive flower features such as only 2 stamens and usually 4 petals of unequal size. The species pictured is a perennial mountain plant with pubescent stems and leaves. In the inflorescence the pedicels are glandular sticky. Note that the corolla has dark purplish veins and the uppermost lobe is considerably wider than the other lobes. The fruit is a heart-shaped capsule with 2 chambers. This alpine beauty can be found near Sexton Glacier.

Many-flowered Stickseed

Borage Family

Hackelia floribunda

Also known as forget-me-not, the many-flowered stickseed receives its name because of the hooks on the nutlets that adhere to fur and clothing when the plant goes to seed. This short-lived biennial grows from 2 to 4 feet tall and bears numerous bright blue flowers on curving flower stalks. The corolla has a short tubular section and then abruptly spreads into 5 lobes. Inside and below the yellow center are 5 small stamens attached to the tube of the corolla. After fertilization, each pistil gives rise to 4 small nutlets with rows of barbed prickles. This species is most apt to be found in moist meadows, streambanks and avalanche paths.

Tall Bluebell; Chimingbell

Borage Family

Mertensia paniculata

This perennial has a clump of leafy stems, each topped by drooping, tubular-shaped flowers. The leaves are alternate and lack hairs. The tubular blossoms are purplish in bud but rapidly turn blue as the corollas open to full size. Five stamens are attached to the inside of the corolla. The fruit consists of 4 wrinkled nutlets. This species occurs along streambanks, wet meadows or seepage areas, especially in the subalpine zone. This species blooms in May in the North Fork lowlands.

Common Harebell

Bluebell Family

Campanula rotundifolia

The generic name of this perennial means little bell and the specific name, *rotundifolia,* refers to the roundish, heart-shaped, basal leaves. While these basal leaves wither early, the narrow, pointed stem leaves remain. A conspicuous feature of the flowers is that, although the buds grow erect, the open blossoms droop or are horizontal, giving protection to the pollen from the rain. Occasionally, completely white or albino flowers will grace the stems of this circumboreal species. Throughout July and August this delicate herb is abundant in the coniferous forest and along roadside cuts.

Alpine Speedwell   1¼x   DO

Many-flowered Stickweed 1¼x   DO

Tall Bluebell   1x   DO

Common Harebell   1x   DO

Wood Forget-me-not

Borage Family

Myosotus sylvatica var. *alpestris*

This periennial is the official state flower of Alaska. The blossoms always tend to be clumped together and each wheel-shaped corolla has a prominent yellow center. The 5 stamens are hidden from view inside the corolla tube. The lance-shaped to linear leaves are covered with long soft hairs. This species grows well in mountain meadows adjacent to Logan Pass and flowers from June through August. The generic name, *Myosotus*, means mouse ear, a reference to the appearance of the leaves of some species. Plants of two other genera are also called forget-me-not: *Eritrichium*, alpine forget-me-not, and *Hackelia*, stickseed.

Blue Camas

Lily Family

Camassia quamash

This member of the lily family is an onion-like plant arising from a bulb which has been used by many Indian tribes as an important food. A leafless flowering stalk reaches a height of about 18 inches and is crowned with a loose cluster of purplish-blue flowers, 1 to 1½ inches in diameter. Harrington also reports that many local Indian wars were fought over the collecting rights to certain blue camas meadows. June is the month to look for blossoms in wet meadows and streambanks. Members of the deer family reportedly feed on the plants in the early spring. This species literally covers fields near East Glacier and St. Mary in some years.

Silky Lupine

Pea Family

Lupinus sericeus

This genus is taxonomically very difficult; as a result, botanists have described about 600 species. The problems with this group arise from natural hybridization, plasticity and glacial recession. The generic name, *Lupinus,* comes from the Latin, *lupus,* wolf, because the plants were believed to rob the soil of nourishment. The lupines, however, really benefit the soil because of their nitrogen-fixing bacteria in root nodules. In spite of their ability to add nitrogen to the soil, some species are potentially dangerous because of alkaloids contained in the leguminous fruits. Silky lupine is probably the most common of our species, widespread from British Columbia to Arizona. It is found in grasslands, sagebrush and low elevation forests.

Common Blue-eyed Grass

Iris Family

Sisyrinchium angustifolium

These miniatures of the iris family will always draw favorable comments. The flattened stems are about 6 to 12 inches tall and are topped with 1 to 5 flowers. Where the 3 sepals and 3 petals join there is usually a yellow center. Note also that each perianth member is tipped with a minute point. The 3 stamens are joined with the style to form a central column. This column plus the inferior ovary are the features that set this plant apart as a member of the iris family. This species grows in wet meadows from sea level to the alpine zone and blooms in June and July.

Wood Forget-me-not 1x   DO

Blue Camas 1¼x   DO

Silky Lupine ¾x   DO

Common Blue-eyed Grass 1¼x   DO

Silky Phacelia

Waterleaf Family

Phacelia sericea

The genus, *Phacelia,* is large and perlexing with at least 150 species in North America. Silky phacelia, however, is one of the easiest to recognize. The leaves are long-petioled and irregular in their pinnate lobes. The dense elongate flower spikes may be up to 9 inches long. The 5 petals are fused at the base forming a saucer. The dark purple stamens extend well beyond the corolla, giving the inflorescence a fuzzy appearance. The specific name, *sericea,* means silky and refers to the silky pubescence covering stems and leaves. This perennial grows in rather dry soils of trails and roadsides from 4,500 to 5,500 feet, and flowers in July and early August.

Dotted Gayfeather

Composite Family

Liatris punctata

This handsome composite occupies dry open places, including open montane forests. Several stiff stems grow up to 2 feet from an underground corm. The lower part of the stem is covered with narrow, stiff leaves. The unusual flower heads consist of 4 to 6 showy disk flowers. Each pistil of a disk flower has 2 purple, twisted appendages which make the entire head resemble a feather. Plains Indians are reported to have consumed the corms as a survival food only. The common name, blazing star, has also been applied to this species, but is more appropriately applied to *Mentzelia laevicaulis.* This specimen was photographed at the buffalo paddock in Waterton Park.

Purple Onion

Lily Family

Allium schoenoprasum

Wild onions have been used for their edible bulbs since ancient times, both in the new and old worlds. The Indians ate the bulbs raw or cooked them with other food. Many mammals, such as bear and elk, also utilize these odoriferous plants. There are about 500 species of onions in the world, and all have the same distinctive flower structure — 3 sepals, 3 petals, 6 stamens and 3 fused carpels. The flowering stem is commonly 6 to 13 inches, and the flower cluster has several tissue-like bracts where the pedicels join the main stem. Flowering begins in June and continues into August at higher elevations.

Parry's Townsendia

Composite Family

Townsendia parryi

The flower heads of *Townsendia* resemble those of *Aster* and *Erigeron,* but undivided and unlobed leaves plus single, large heads at the ends of short stems help to separate this *Townsendia* from these confusing species. The stem is covered with appressed, coarse hairs. The spatulate-shaped leaves are 1 to 2 inches long, and most of them form a crowded rosette at ground level. This species inhabits grasslands and dry woodlands on the east side of the Park. This species blooms very early near Kiowa Junction.

Silky Phacelia   1x   DO

Dotted Gayfeather   1x   DO

Purple Onion   ¾x   DO

Parry's Townsendia   1x   DO

Leafy Aster

Aster foliaceus

Composite Family

In the genus, *Aster,* we find many variable species which intergrade with one another; even a plant taxonomist would be cautious about estimating the number of species in the two parks (14 species are listed in the checklist). The species illustrated is highly variable with broad non-toothed leaves and numerous lavender to violet rays. The plants reproduce both by seed and by rhizomes. Most species begin to flower in late summer and continue to blossom until they are killed by frost.

Common Selfheal; Healall

Prunella vulgaris

Mint Family

Common selfheal was once esteemed for healing wounds, but now it is considered only as a refreshing beverage which can be made by chopping and boiling the leaves. The flowers are usually purple to pink. The corolla is 2-lipped, the upper lip forming a hood. The calyx is usually purplish and covered with long hairs. There are 4 stamens in two sets. Like other members of the mint family, the stems are square and fitted with opposite leaves. The plant inhabits stream banks, lake shores and flowers in July or August. Disturbed areas, such as trailsides and roadsides, are also favorite sites for this plant.

Explorers Bog Gentian

Gentiana calycosa

Gentian Family

The showy flowers of this beautiful gentian are pleated and twisted in bud. The widely spreading lobes alternate with the cleft extensions of the pleats or folds. The stamens are epipetalous and do not protrude from the tube of the corolla. This low herb of the mountains has many erect stems, each with numerous ovate, opposite leaves and a single blossom. The genus, *Gentiana,* is a large one with dozens of species in the arctic and temperate regions. Moist rocky soils near timberline are good places to look for this flower. Siyeh Pass Trail has many good sites as does Stoney Indian Pass Trail.

Sky-pilot; Skunk Plant

Polemonium viscosum

Phlox Family

Throughout the Rocky Mountains, sky-pilot is symbolic of high altitudes, and it grows on scree slopes and in protected rock crevices. The leaves with numerous roundish leaflets are sticky and carry a skunk-like odor which will adhere to shoes and clothes of the mountaineer. The corolla is funnel-shaped with 5 expanded lobes. The 5 stamens have brilliant orange pollen which contrasts markedly with the blue to lavender petals, forming a recognition sign to the alpine bee pollinators. Depending on elevation, blooms will occur from June through August. This species is common on Carthew Pass and in W.N.P.

Leafy Aster 1x   DO

Common Selfheal ⅞x   DO

Explorers Bog Gentian 1x   DO

Sky-pilot 1¼x   DO

Sugarbowl; Hairy Clematis

Buttercup Family

Clematis hirsutissima

This striking, herbaceous plant commonly reaches 1 to 2 feet in height. The flower has no petals and the purple, petaloid sepals are obscured on the outer surface by a covering of cobwebby hairs. Many stamens and pistils are enclosed by the perianth bowl. The fruits of sugarbowl are achenes with long feathery styles. The leaves are opposite and are two to four times pinnately dissected. Other local names are leather flower and vase flower. The plant often grows with the big sagebrush and blooms in late June or early July.

Showy Fleabane

Composite Family

Erigeron speciosus

The specific name, *speciosus,* means showy, and well describes the brightly colored heads of this handsome species. Showy fleabane stems may be up to 25 inches high and bear several flower heads, each with from 70 to 150 slender, whitish to purplish ray flowers. The tubular disk flowers are yellow-orange. Separating species of *Erigeron* from *Aster* can be frustrating, but generally, many fleabanes flower earlier in the summer season than asters. Also the ray flowers of *Erigeron* are generally more numerous and narrower. The plant can be found in dry to moist soil in open, wooded areas.

Upland Larkspur

Buttercup Family

Delphinium nuttallianum

The generic name, *Delphinium,* is derived from the latin *delphinius* meaning dolphin, a reference to a dolphin-like shaped flower in some species. The upper sepal in this genus extends backward into a prominent spur. The spur sepal plus 4 other sepals expand to reveal 4 smaller petals of lighter color. The herbage and seeds of larkspurs possess alkaloids poisonous to man and animals. The plant is commonly less than 2 feet tall and the stem develops from clusters of tuberous roots. Hummingbirds are frequent visitors to the flowers. This species is widely distributed from sagebrush areas to mountain valleys and even to the alpine zone on dry, rocky ridges.

Sugarbowl ¾x

Showy Fleabane ¾x

Upland Larkspur 1x

Shrubby Penstemon

Figwort Family

Penstemon fruticosus

Fruticosus, meaning shrub-like, appropriately describes this semi-shrub with trailing leafy stems. The leaves are semi-evergreen which means only a few leaves turn reddish in the fall, and later fall off. The flowers are up to 2 inches long and generally blue-lavender. The lower portion of the tubular corolla is lined with long, white hairs. When the corolla is opened lengthwise and viewed under a hand lens, the attached anthers are seen to be densely white-haired. This species is common locally on rocky alpine ledges. Lyall's penstemon *(P. lyallii)* a similar appearing plant, is abundant on the scree slopes between Siyeh Bend and Logan Pass.

Jones Columbine; Blue Columbine

Buttercup Family

Aquilegia jonesii

One of the most delightful experiences for the mountaineer or trail hiker is to cross a limestone scree slope and discover this small perennial (up to 4 inches) with its large flowers. Both the sepals and petals are deep blue or purplish. The 5 petals have long tubes or spurs extending straight backward which are often filled with nectar. There are many stamens and 5 pistils. All the leaves of this species are in tufts at ground level, and the crowded leaflets are strongly pubescent. Blossoms are found from June to August. The Smithsonian Institution lists this species as one which is threatened, yet some botanists disagree with this classification. It has been reported on Siyeh Pass and on the east slope of Mt. Wilbur. It has also been seen on Dawson Pass, Pitamakan Pass and Gable Pass. In 1977, white-flowered specimens were found on Siyeh Pass.

Alpine Aster

Composite Family

Aster alpigenus var. *haydenii*

In the two parks there may be about 14 species of asters, many of which hybridize freely. Even the specialist has difficulty separating the species, and all parts of the plant including the roots must be studied. Aster species are not easily distinguished from daisies *(Erigeron)*. On close examination daisies are found to have 50 or more ray flowers. This dwarf aster is always found high in the mountains clinging to life in cracks of weathering rocks. In the flowering head there are 10 to 40 ray flowers about ½ inch long. The involucral bracts, as in all asters, form several overlapping rows of different lengths and may be purplish. The basal leaves are somewhat folded.

Shrubby Penstemon   1x   DO

Jones Columbine   1x   DO

Alpine Aster ¾x   RJS

Fuzzytongue Penstemon

Penstemon eriantherus

The penstemons of the two parks, as well as those of the Rocky Mountains, constitute a confusing and taxonomically difficult genus. In all species the petals are united into a long corolla tube with 5 spreading lobes, the lower 3 forming a landing platform for pollinating insects. Four of the 5 stamens are fertile and lie against the upper portion of the corolla. The fifth stamen is sterile, and in the species illustrated, the sterile stamen extends beyond the opening of the corolla. Note the conspicuous hairs on this tongue-like structure. This species grows on dry, rocky and sandy hills at moderate elevations.

Pasque Flower; Wild Crocus

Buttercup Family

Anemone nuttalliana

Close examination of pasque flower blossoms reveals some unique features. The petaloid sepals are 1-1½ inches long, colored purple, lavender or even white, and have an outer hairy surface. Numerous stamens surround numerous pistils which, upon maturation, produce a cluster of fruits resembling a lion's beard, hence another common name — lionsbeard. The whorl of leaves on the stem below the flower, plus 5 or 6 sepals, are characteristic of the genus. This widespread species grows in prairies to mountain meadows where the soil is well-drained. The name, *anemone,* is derived from the Greek word for wind. This species is very common in the foothills of the east side. Most of the plants bloom in May.

Common Butterwort

Bladderwort Family

Pinguicula vulgaris

This circumboreal species is found on calcareous soils by cold springs or seepages. The compact rosette of leaves have inrolled edges and sticky glands that trap and digest small insects, thus providing the plant with nitrogen and other nutrients. The flowers are solitary at the ends of leafless stems up to 6 inches tall. The corolla is 2-lipped with one part prolonged into a basal spur which produces nectar. In many ways members of this family are like the figwort family except they have only 2 stamens and differ in details of the pistil. Look for this species along the trail from Logan Pass to Granite Park Chalet and on the trail to Grinnell Glacier.

Naked Broomrape

Broomrape Family

Orobanche uniflora

All members of this family are parasites on the roots of other plants. Since these plants have no chlorophyll, they cannot manufacture their own food; instead they must draw nourishment from some host plant that has the ability to carry on photosynthesis. The leaves of broomrapes are reduced to alternate scales. The pubescent flowers are 2-lipped and contain 4 stamens in two pairs. Since only the blossoms and their pedicels appear above the ground level, the plant is often missed by visitors. These plants have been seen on the west shore of Waterton Lake and along the North Fork River.

Fuzzytongue Penstemon 1x DO

Pasque Flower 1x DO

Common Butterwort 1x DO

Naked Broomrape ⅞x DO

Striped Coralroot

Corallorhiza striata

Coralroot orchids are devoid of the green pigment, chlorophyll, and cannot manufacture their own food. They are completely dependent on a group of saprophytic fungi in the duff of the coniferous forest. Thus the coralroots live as parasites on the saprophytic fungi; and, therefore, they can survive in very shady habitats since they do not need light for photosynthesis. The broad lower petal (lip) is almost completely purple, but the upper petals and sepals have 3 red-purple stripes.

Spotted Coralroot

Orchid Family

Corallorhiza maculata

Most members of the orchid family, including the coralroots, are becoming increasingly rare as man progressively destroys their moist forest habitats. Transplanting to the garden should not be attempted because the coral-like rhizomes are associated with a complex group of fungi that are found only in natural sites. Slender asparagus-like stems appear in late June and early July and quickly develop racemes from which the flowers open. The specific name, *maculata,* means spotted, and is given because of the purple to brown spots on the 3-lobed, white lip of the flower. Under a hand lens it is obvious that the flower is incredibly adapted for cross-pollination by insects. This species has been seen in the North Fork and in the Belly River area.

Woodland Pinedrops

Wintergreen Family

Pterospora andromedea

The reddish-brown stem may reach a height of 3½ feet, and it is covered with sticky hairs. The leaves are small and scale-like on the lower half of the stem. Since the herbaceous stem and leaves lack the pigment, chlorophyll, the plant cannot produce its own food; it therefore takes its nourishment from other sources. Careful research has shown that this plant lives as a parasite on soil fungi. The urn-shaped, nodding flowers have a 5-parted calyx and a united corolla. The fruits of the raceme mature into brown capsules that release great quantities of seed. Pinedrops inhabits the coniferous forest. It grows at widely scattered locations, and alert visitors on the North Fork Truck Trail will see it.

Fringed Pinesap

Wintergreen Family

Hypopitys monotropa

The name, *Hypopitys,* comes from the Greek words *hypo,* meaning beneath, and *pitys,* meaning pine tree — a specific reference to the habitat. The leaves of pinesap are reduced to small scales, and there is no chlorophyll in the plant. This means that the nourishment for the plant must come from some other source, in this case the root system is really parasitic on the saprophytic fungi growing in the forest humus. The perianth members are 3 to 5 merous, and the stamens are usually twice as many as the petals.

Striped Coralroot 1¼x DO

Spotted Coralroot 1x DO

Woodland Pinedrops ⅞x DO

Fringed Pinesap ¾x DO

Bronzebells
Stenanthium occidentale
The generic name stems from the Greek words, *stenos,* and *anthos,* meaning narrow flower in reference to the narrow perianth parts. The bell-like flowers are pendant, reddish or greenish-yellow; the individual petals have pointed tips that roll back, exposing the delicate interior of the blossom. Grass-like leaves, up to a foot long, emerge from an onion-like bulb. The plant grows mostly in alpine or subalpine regions in wet cliffs, rock crevices and even meadows. Flowering occurs during June and July.

Mountain Sorrel
Buckwheat Family
Oxyria digyna
The mountain sorrel is one of the most wide-spread of all alpine plants, growing around the world in the high latitudes and extending southward along the mountain ranges. The greenish to red flowers have 4 sepals, 6 stamens and are apparently wind pollinated. Ample fruit and seed is produced each year, and these fruits dangle from slender stems like Japanese lanterns. The succulent, acid leaves and young stems are edible and satisfying for quenching thirst. This plant is high in vitamin C and is frequently eaten in the Arctic by the Eskimos.

Common Cattail
Cattail Family
Typha latifolia
The common cattail is probably the most famous of all edible wild plants. Rootstocks, young shoots and young flower inflorescences can be utilized as delicious wild food. The tall brown "cat's tail" is composed of thousands of minute female flowers, each one being little more than a single pistil. Directly above the pistillate spike, temporary staminate flowers appear. When the pollen is shed, these upper flowers disappear. Rootstocks are high in starch content, and this carbohydrate can be extracted to yield a flour comparable to that made from wheat or corn. The Indians used the down (bracts from the flowers) for bedding and as diapers.

Giant Helleborine
Orchid Family
Epipactis gigantea
This perennial herb, also called stream orchid, is so named because of the height to which it grows and its superficial resemblance to the hellebore. The flowers are in a raceme with leaflike bracts. There are usually only two or three prime flowers on each stem, as the lower ones wither while the uppermost are still in bud. Width of the blossoms varies from ½ to ¾ inch. Under a hand lens the bilaterally symmetrical flowers reveal a very intricate makeup with delicate veins running through the petals.

Bronzebells ¾x   DO

Mountain Sorrel ½x   DO

Common Cattail ¼x   RJS

Giant Helleborine 1x   RJS

Parts Of A Flower

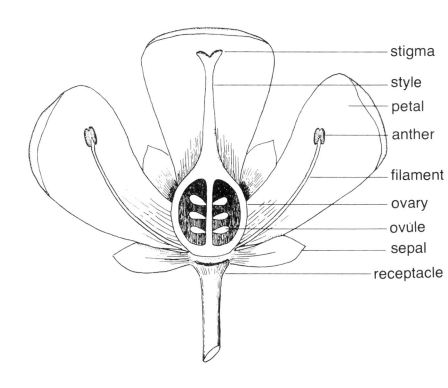

- stigma
- style
- petal
- anther
- filament
- ovary
- ovule
- sepal
- receptacle

Glossary

Achene – A small, dry fruit which does not open by itself.

Androecium – The collective term for all the stamens in one flower.

Anther – The pollen-bearing part of the stamen.

Biennial – A plant which completes its life cycle and dies in two years.

Bilabiate – Having two lips; referring to calyx or corolla.

Bract – A modified leaf associated with a flower.

Calyx – All of the sepals of a flower considered collectively

Capsule – A dry, dehiscent (splitting open) fruit composed of more than one carpel.

Carpel – The basic unit of a pistil; the pod of a pea is a good example.

Circumboreal – Occuring all the way around the northern latitudes.

Corolla – A collective term referring to the petals of a flower.

Deciduous – Falling off after completion of the normal function.

Disk flower – A central flower of a composite inflorescence (such as the center of a sunflower).

Floret – An individual small flower of a definite cluster.

Foliate – Referring to leaflets of a compound leaf.

Follicle – A dry fruit formed from a single carpel, splitting open along one edge only.

Inflorescence – A flower bearing branch or system of branches.

Involucral – Referring to a set of bracts beneath an inflorescence.

Node – A point on a stem where a leaf is (or has been) attached.

Pappus – A modified calyx, usually composed of bristles or awns and always associated with composite family.

Pedicel – The stalk of a single flower.

Peduncle – The common stalk of a flower cluster.

Perianth – The collective term applied to the sepals and petals of a flower.

151

Perennial – Living year after year.

Petaloid – Petal-like

Petiole – A leaf stalk.

Pinnate – Having two rows of parts or appendages along an axis, like barbs on a feather.

Pistillate flower – A flower bearing one or more pistils but no stamens.

Pollination – Transfer of the pollen from the anther to the stigma by such agents as wind, insects and birds.

Pubescence – The various types of hairs that cover the surface of a plant.

Raceme – An elongated inflorescence with a single main axis along which stalked flowers are arranged.

Ray flowers – The strap-shaped marginal flowers of the composite family; each ray flower is complete with corolla and essential organs.

Receptacle – The tip of a floral axis, bearing the parts of a flower.

Salverform – Having a slender tube and an abruptly spreading set of corolla lobes.

Silique — An elongated capsule of the mustard family.

Staminate flower – Having one or more stamens but no pistils.

Succulent – Fleshy and juicy.

Umbel – An inflorescence in which the pedicels radiate from a single point like the spokes of an umbrella.

Villous — Covered with long, soft hairs.

Selected References

Beetle, Alan A. 1970. *Recommended plant names*. Research Jour. 31, Agric. Research Sta., University of Wyoming, Laramie.

Craighead, John J., Frank C. Craighead, and Ray J. Davis. 1963. *A Field Guide to Rocky Mountain Wildflowers*. Houghton-Mifflin Co., Boston.

Hardin, James., and Jay M. Arena. 1969. *Human Poisoning from Native and Cultivated Plants*. Duke University Press, Durham, No. Carolina.

Harrington, H.D. 1967. *Edible Native Plants of the Rocky Mountains*. University of New Mexico Press, Albuquerque.

Hitchcock, C. Leo, and Arthur Cronquist. 1973. *Flora of the Pacific Northwest*. University of Washington Press, Seattle.

Kessell, Stephen R. 1974. *Checklist of Vascular Plants of Glacier National Park, Montana*. The Glacier National Park Natural History Association, West Glacier, Montana.

Kirk, Donald R. 1970. *Wild Edible Plants of the Western United States*. Naturegraph, Healdsburg, California.

Long, John C. 1965. *Native Orchids of Colorado*. Denver Museum of Natural History, Pictorial No. 16.

Luer, Carlyle A. 1975. *The Native Orchids of the United States and Canada*. New York Botanical Garden, New York.

Rickett, Harold W. 1973. *Wildflowers of the United States*. Vol. 6. McGraw-Hill Co., New York.

Weber, William A. 1976. *Rocky Mountain Flora*. Colorado Associated University Press, Boulder, Colorado.

Weiner, Michael A. 1972. *Earth Medicine – Earth Foods*. Collier Books, New York.

Index

155

157